A Life Lived
Inspired
To Share With
Many

Claudia W. Salassidis

Dedication

To my late Parents & Siblings

To my Family especially, Aunty Norma and Yvonne my sister.

To My Church Families & My Friends Christine, Nicole, Citira & Sherry

And the countless people who walked with me & to those who are still in my life today

Shira and Shelley, my therapists

But most of all
To my God
My Husband Perry and My Son Asher
The three love of my life
I would like to say
Thanks to everyone

Acknowledgment

There are truly no words, neither mine nor those of anyone who knows you, that could fully capture the depth of our gratitude, appreciation, and heartfelt indebtedness to a woman of your extraordinary caliber. From my earliest days in kindergarten through to adulthood, you have stood by me and my family during our most trying times, offering unwavering support, compassion, and generosity. You are a rare gem, singular in spirit, radiant in heart. There is so much I wish to say, yet no dictionary could ever contain the words sufficient to reflect the kindness, love, and compassion, and admiration you so richly inspired. Your heart shines with the brilliance of the sun, illuminating the lives of all those fortunate enough to know you.

Only God in his infinite grace can reward you in measure with the greatness of your gift, for it surpasses anything this world could ever offer. No pen, no paper could ever encompass the overflowing gratitude we feel. On behalf of my family, I thank you deeply for the love, encouragement, and generous support you have extended to us time and again. Your boundless kindness touches not only those close to you, but even strangers, and it never goes unnoticed. For all of this and so much more…. I dedicate this book especially to you, with all our love.

We love you with all our heart. Aunty Norma.

Contents

UNFOLDING GOD'S BLESSINGS AND THE CHALLENGES I FACED IN LIFE AS I GREW AND MATURED

UNFOLDED

The purpose of this book is to offer my readers the tools and strategies to overcome difficult times.

I believe in the unique power of personal

storytelling

so, I've chosen to share my own story

I hope my book brings you enjoyment and valuable

Insights

———————————————————

———————————————

———————————

————

——

—

GOD BLESS YOU ALL

Introduction
My Generation Up-Bringing

I never thought I would be the first one in my family to want to write a book about my life. I have wanted to write this book since I moved to America but never did. But after living my life with my immediate family, I started to feel stronger and stronger about writing it. Right now, I feel like it's the right time to put it all together. Most of all, I have to give God the praise for not allowing me to detour from writing this book to help others.

Although I grew up mostly in North America, I decided to start writing from my humble beginnings in Jamaica because that's where I was molded into the person I am today. Living in North America has allowed me to meet some of the most wonderful and amazing people who have helped me to become the woman I am today. I do have a lot of church friends who would invite me to their homes sometime after church or during the week to just chat as friends usually do.

Some of my friends are in different provinces in Canada or other States in America. Some of them I would love to see and recap the days we lost. However, I would love to see my best friend, Citira Sittal, who I went to high school with. She never stopped searching for me until she located me. My friend, when you read my book, I want to let you know that you are a good

1

friend, as that's what true friends do. Friends never stop until they know the other friend is able to connect. Thank God that he spared my life to come to the realization that I have a true friend from my high school days. I was in America when my friend was trying to find me, but she found me living in Canada.

After moving to Canada, God allowed me to meet the most wonderful man in the world. He has been through so much with me and never once complained. Just like everyone, we all have our good and bad days. However, it has made us stronger, allowing us to talk about what we need to work on and what we are grateful for. To sum it up, we're never going to leave each other. Having God in our lives has kept both of us together. Throughout our experiences, I have matured from a simple, naïve girl to a wonderful, trustworthy woman who truly loves from the heart, and no, I am not perfect. We both aren't.

On another note, there are people that I have met in my life's journey that meant me no good. My friend, who found me after looking for me for a long time, gave me the encouragement to assure me that a true friend does last forever. To those who can relate to this paragraph in my book, I hope you will cherish those friends who care enough to touch your heart the way my good friend did.

Nonetheless, I also want to let you know that there are many friends who would behave in the nicest way when they are around you, but behind your back, they would rip you apart as if they were ripping a leaf from a hated page of a book, to show how they were really feeling about you. I have, as well, so-called friends who have ripped me apart, as stated above. Sometimes even discussing me around their dinner tables, during rides, laughing as they talked about me in the worst way, and sometimes even while I'm in the same room. All I could do, in those times is to ask God for a forgiving heart.

Just imagine how I felt at that moment. The moment would go over and over in my head. I would cry sometimes and would feel very sad. Thinking that I truly believe they were my friends. I had to learn the hard fact that those were really not my friends. If you have encountered friends like those, just know that you don't have to harbor hate and malice. For me, I have learned that love conquers all hateful behavior. My encouragement is that you don't have to reciprocate the same bad behavior to the people who will do everything to tear you down.

Therefore, my take on such behavior is that Love conquers all hate. Hatred stirs up conflict, but Love covers all wrong flows over to comfort you in times of need.

Does love really conquer hate?

This is the thing, only love possesses the remarkable power to drive out hate and bring about transformative change in the world.

"Love is a force that transcends boundaries, heals wounds, and unites even the most divided of hearts."

When we choose love over hate, we open ourselves to the possibility of understanding, compassion, and forgiveness. Through love, we can break the cycle of hatred and create a more harmonious and compassionate society. Love has the capacity to touch the deepest parts of our souls, enabling us to see the humanity in others, even when they may appear as adversaries. When we respond to hate with love, we demonstrate strength and resilience. *(Oct 14,2023) "Russell Boschetto"* This is so true, and I could not have said it better.

Have I experienced a time of hate? Yes, I have and had hated silently for a long time. Because of others who were jealous of me for the many talents I was blessed with and those talents, I did them well. E.g. "Rising in jobs". God has blessed me with many gifts that some people I knew wanted to do the things I do, but were not able to do them as well as I did. E.g. In singing. At times, I was randomly called to render songs at many functions, which I did by the grace of God at all times. This was my gift from God, and I did it to praise him at all times, never to be seen or be praised by others.

People would tell others that I thought I was better than other people, but I won't call names as my love still remains the same. No one can take this gift that God gave me, which is to love even through emotional pain. I have never thought, at any time in my life, that I was better than anyone. I confidently can say I'm the least, when I look at others. All I was able to do in life was what God has given me and I have always done it all, with the help of God.

I also believe that God has blessed and has given me the gift and ability to do many things that I thought I was not capable of doing. E.g. "Writing this book." All we have to do is to give God the praise and that's what I did every time he used me to give him praise in song or anything. I humbly claim all God's blessings on my life and believe with all my heart that I can do whatever he set before me. No need to be jealous.

One would think I would learn from it and keep my distance. The truth is, I cannot in my heart hurt anyone or feel hate or wish the worst for people. I don't have it in me because of God dwelling in me. It's all for his glory. I have learned, after I gave my life to God, that if I wish the worst on others, I would be wishing the worst on myself and perhaps my family as well. In any situation that I find myself in, I just cannot hate people. I reject harboring such feelings in my heart. Even when some try to taint my reputation, my Christian life and most of all my inner-self.

I love people in general such that there was never an option in my life growing up, to hate. However, I must say, and will share that, I was driven for three years in my life's journey to feel somewhat of a hate towards someone who did the worst to me. At the same time, saying to me that they were my friend. To my readers in general, I just don't like the way people talk about others and sometimes about me and I guess some of my readers have also experienced what I am talking about. I know with God, I can choose, in any situation to concur to love and to concur not to hate.

It took me a while, but I kept at it until the anger with hate turned to love. So, I encourage myself, and now to you I'll say, just stay strong as he, God is our (my)refuge and strength. I can love and now, always willing and ready to forgive and never to resent anyone, no matter what happens throughout my journey in life.

Have I experienced moments of lows in my life? Yes, I have! When I was younger and even as an adult. I did not love myself enough in my earlier stage in life. I had self-esteem issues. I loved people more than I loved myself and felt I had or had to cave into their requests at time. Why I have to justify everything I say and do? I cannot figure it out, even to this moment, as I'm writing this book.

However, Luke 6 v **27-30** assist me with the life I live in God. Saying **27**, "But I say unto you which hear, love your enemies, do good to them which hate you, **28** bless them that curse you, and pray for them which despitefully use you. **29** And unto him that smiteth thee on the one cheek offer also the other; and he that taketh away thy cloke forbid not to take thy coat also. **30** Give to every man that asketh of thee; and of him that taketh away thy goods ask them not again. **31** And as ye would that men should do to you, do ye also to them likewise.

32 For if ye love them which love you, what thank have ye? Is that to you? For sinners also love those that love them. **33** And if ye do good to them which do good to you, what thank have ye? For sinners also do even the same. **34** And if ye lend to them of whom ye hope to receive, what thank have ye? For sinners, to receive as much again.

But love ye your enemies, and do good, and lend, hoping for nothing again; And your reward shall be great, and ye shall be the children of the Highest: for he is kind unto the unthankful and to the evil. 36 Be ye therefore merciful, as you Father also is merciful. In judging others, I have learned that God wants me, to not judge, so I would not be judged. I should not condemn, and I will not be condemned. I should forgive, and I will be forgiven. Give, and it will be given to me. And not only given but in good measure, pressed down, shaken together and running over, will be poured into your lap. For with the measure you use, it will be measured to you.

Because I trust God and his words, I believe, at the end of the day, I rather bear the bad in all situations of my life, even to this day. Others may not believe in the bible the way I do, and you don't have to agree with me in the way I live my life and have my life governed by God's words. So, keep on reading as there are some inciteful lessons as you continue to read my life which I believe is worth sharing. Nevertheless, no one has to follow my way of life, but what I would like you to take away from all this is that love, giving, and sharing does conquer all situations. This is just another of my life experiences.

Twice, I had a rude awakening that I will never want to experience again. Roommate issues. I will never live with any roommate/s again in life. To encourage my readers, I would say not all people are rude, hurtful, and disrespectful. However, my heart aches to say we have some people that have had troubling lives and makes it their goal to make others pay for the crappy life they believe they had or have to endure.

Just do your homework and be true to yourself and to others who are genuine family or friends. However, put your antenna on when searching for someone to share a space with you. There are some who will take you for a ride, and you will have to put your guard up. Others can be the best decision ever, but the key is to do your due diligence when wanting to share space with others.

Regarding issues that you face that are dire, find a professional, family, or a true friend who can help before you let the wrong person into your inner-self, as one day, we will be judged by God alone for the way we treat each other. Why I say the above is I have lived with few friends and have had the worst falling out which had me crying for days. To be honest, still to this day, I cannot understand why people are like that and the cause of their bad, destructive behaviors. Stay true to yourself and be the best you.

Due to that experience, I can encourage my readers that, in life, you have to love yourself first, as love starts from within. Beside loving my creator, I or we have to love ourselves in the process of doing anything in life. One of the things to remember when remembering sad encounters with so-called friends and destructive family members is that "loving you or loving one-self equates to loving others". That's having the love that comes only from God.

Not loving yourself sometimes gives your enemy/s an opportunity to abuse you. (The saying: Actions speak louder than words, it's a true saying) watch for the signs/actions, as it does not lie, it does matter and most of all, don't forget to read the eyes, as it holds the deepness of the inner emotions from the heart. To be honest, the phrase has kept me on my toes after my many encounters dealing with some of the people in my life. I have met, some people in my life that has hurt me to my core. Sometimes, I am too firm when speaking the truth, therefore causing many to distort my actions.

Nevertheless, I stay firm in remembering God's words in Isaiah 43: 2-3 When you pass through the waters, I will be with you; and when you pass through the rivers, they will not sweep over you. When you walk through the fire, you will not be burned; the flames will not set you ablaze, for I am the Lord, your God, the Holy One of Israeli, your Savior. I trust God to take care of me every day in life. I also would like my readers to know that I have good and bad days, even when I put my trust in God. I am as human as anyone living on this earth. But what I am saying is that not because we share those rough days sometimes, we should cast ourselves to the wolves of the world. No! What I'm saying is that we should examine our day-to-day interaction with others and use it to choose wisely in situations, friendships and in how we want to live our lives.

When others choose me to be their friend, I find that it seems to frustrate others, as they sometimes would say, what about them? It would infuriate some, as they can't see how a friend or friends, both male and female of mine, would choose me to be their friend or liking someone like me. People think that I am boring and that they are better-looking than me. I have heard some saying, what about them or what's there in me, that I can be dating and marrying my now husband. I had to be strong and to have courage with God's grace upon my life. It was not easy, but I'm reminded that God knows all things, and he will help me with things I have overheard people saying about me.

The hated encounters, sometimes, were disturbing. On one encounter in a dangerous situation, someone told me, while coming up close to my face, pointing their finger, telling me that I couldn't find a black man, and that's why I had to accept a white man. Others would lash out at me or was cheeky toward me. To this day, I still can't understand why! For it seems things I say or do, make some people get angry at me. E.g. In jobs that I have had, some criticize me with other friends, co-workers, and employees and would be intentionally curt, as those people would think, that I demonstrate a prejudicing or reprimanding persona.

If you my readers have ever experience being around people who hate you for no reason? Pay it no attention as we can't change all people, but we can be a beacon to those who desire a change. That was how I handle people of such behavior.

Let me open up by saying, since I have known and heard my voice-on-voice machine messages, I realize that I have a raspy/dysphonia voice tone, and because my voice is misleading to some people, I would be judged harshly for it many times. Saying I was being rough and rude to them. I can love my enemies and don't have to worry about them as the older I get, and the more I mature and with God directing my life, I have allowed myself to be at peace through the stormy waves. I would ask God to help me to continue loving people instead of hating them. "A phrase I will use a lot in my book".

Hate is a disease. It will control your head and heart and eat you up, spitting you out and eventually destroying your life. I encourage all my readers to stand tall and fight, take back your life, and choose to keep their minds healthy. Do not beat up yourself or try to change yourself for others; unless you really need to because you have to, but it should only be for you, if you are going to learn from the changes you will make to enhance you for the better.

For me, I changed my life only because I love God and to love God is to love others according to his book. You have to love those who you can see (who are people) before you can love who you cannot see (who is God), and most of all, God is love. So, love yourself as well because that love will spill out of you unto others. I had to change for him and me, so that I can receive the pure love that only God can give to whomever asked of him, so that we can love like he would want us to.

Nevertheless, just lift yourself up and be the best you can for yourself before the eyes of God. Never please a friend/s from both genders. Please God for who he is and what he stands for. People will say bad things about you or hateful things in rage, meaning you are no good. But!! Amidst all that you are going through, stay strong. You will one day Rise from the struggle of it all. "In whatever you are going through."

Believe in yourself always, and embrace who you are, and to encourage you, I would say, if you are not strong enough, seek help, and when you get that help, do the homework that you are asked to do or that's assigned to you. It will help you crawl out of your situations/pain and even your frustrations, your experience will help you to grow and to move forward. Just continue to seek help and if the professionals' help at the time of your need is not working out for you, just ask for a second opinion.

When you feel healthy mentally, physically, or emotionally enough, try to focus on shaking your dusty pass, so you can rise like a stallion and welcome the new you.

Living your new life and a new way of living it. (Mine is

when I gave my life to God) And since then, even when things aren't going well, I evoke every time and now, it's my way to live my life. Also, for me, it has been the best choice I could ever make for my life.

That's my decision, it doesn't have to be yours. You make the choice. I will not tell anyone to follow my way of living my life, but what I will say is that this is my life, and I am hoping my book will help you make the best decisions for yourself in difficult moments in life while living on earth. I believe that God has allowed me to write this book to someone out there… in a world filled with many crises.

It's hard to want to trust God, as God is the one who knows all things and who we should be able to put our trust in, but most of all, the God, who can make everything be for the better. I know God can make things that are impossible be possible, or painfully hard to deal with situations to work out for the best when we trust him to handle our situations for us. Also, one of the greatest heart-wrenching pains is when our loved ones die unexpectedly. Or to forgive others, when they deliberately take our loved ones from us. It's really hard to forgive in a scenario of such selfishness. Sometimes, we lose our loved ones to unpredictable circumstances that can be heart-wrenching.

Just keep strong.

Nonetheless, I still trust him as I believe amidst all these things that are happening to us, there is an answer to what and why things are the way they are, and often we still sometimes have no answers to it all. Yet, I still believe God is my Answer for everything that I go through. As he told me, in his words that he will never leave me nor forsake me. I also believe that I have won the best gift ever when I found God, and I'm able to be given his Grace, Mercy and blessings especially when I see another day lived. Or every day to see a new morning.

Let me open up a little now about my twenty-fifteen breakdown. In that year and after for eight years, I have had my physical, mental, emotional, and most of all my spiritual state questioned in so many ways.

Some friends and people that I was close to tested me for many years in my time of mental desolation, nevertheless. I had to embrace those moments with courage and faith, knowing I could not hate or not speak to people. I had to represent the child of God that he made me to be. There are moments, while going through my most difficult ones, that I had to be strong while being talked about once again. What makes it hard at times is when I am openly talked about as others pass me by once again. I was vulnerable at that time, and I was stripped of every emotion to keep me living. To sum it up, I was very fragile. However, I'm truly grateful for the grace that he has bestowed up on me and my family in my crisis. It's like people cannot stop talking about me. I just let them.

Thank God, I gave him my life a long time ago and have walked this road so many times (having people talking about me). Did I get over it? Yes! Eventually. But not without some sobbing, painful tears. I, however, am happy to know that I could not cross these torturous roads without God's. But most of all, I also would like to say that this process keeps me humble.

The more years I go through the experience I continue to grow to trust God more, and the more I am able to let him take care of the things I have no control over. It was great that I had my family, real friends, and church family who cared deeply for me, but, sometimes, I'm dying inside knowing I just wanted to die and did not want to be around in this world anymore. It was really tough to deal with.

Even though I am a Christian, I am first human and a human who was really in the darkest tunnel that seemed to have no end. My readers understand that being a Christian does not mean you won't go through troublesome times. What it means is that I/you would not be left alone to succumb to our situation. God is real and rains on the good and bad of people. So that none of us can say he favors anyone more than the other. I chose to have God to help me get through it all. Mostly, what helped me week by week, month by month, and year by year is that I had to do the work to get better. No one can do what you have to do for yourself.

I know even serving God, one still has to do the work for a breakthrough! Depression, Anxiety, OCDs, Alcoholics, Drug addicts, and even the struggles of life on a whole. etc. You have to do the work to succeed. Don't crumble, but remain intact and pull yourself together. Did I want to stop and give up?

Yes! Again, I have felt like that many times. However, my determination was to keep working on myself. I, maybe not you, know that God is bigger than all my problems, and all I could and still do is to keep my trust in him. When I talked about doing the work, I mean that I had to ask God daily and had to let him give me the strength to draw closer to him and to the goal I dream of, which was and now still is, to keep getting better and better every day mentally and emotionally. Never forget that admitting that you need help is not failure but is having great strength.

I will say to my readers once again that there are times, and many of a times, I cried a lot. I was also waking up in my sleep because I just could not function. My anxiety was high, and My life meant nothing, more so after the accident in twenty fifteen. I had a body that was in pain constantly and was on so many different medications. I was also tired, mentally and was physically drained daily, even when I wasn't doing anything but sleeping, which was a lot. It was hard to keep on functioning. I can now say that the one thing uncaring people in my state of mind could not do, was to strip me of my inner soul. Why? My soul and life belong to God, who knows me best inside and out and loves me unconditionally as I am fearfully and wonderfully made.

When others fail me, he will never fail me. I just had to stay on the narrow path and be true to God and myself that he would guide me along the steep and bumpy rides that I've been riding. The painful years passed by, and I'm still going through it, yes! So many times. The bumps in life sometimes would and still rock my life's journey and probably yours too; don't let it!

I continued to press on, and I say to you, too, keep pressing on as well. However, if it requires outside help, then seek for the help as I did. Because of the state I was in, and because all that I was experiencing at the time was draining me, I had to seek professional help and I was getting help for many years, to be exact eight years. With their help, I was able to write this book as I was cognitively suffering from brain fog for years and was unable to find words to speak cohesively and to feel alive.

Some of my treatments I have to say, was what I needed most, and have helped me to get back to the Claudia I was and the person I wanted to be, which was to have no pain, mentally, physically, and somewhat to be able to get better, as the months and years goes by. I am still working on myself daily, and is getting there. With that said, I took the courage to walk while holding many hands.

Thank God for choosing them all. Some are still working with me to this day. They are the best team ever. Later on in my book I will talk more about the help they rendered to me. Most of all, the help of my wonderful husband, my understanding son, and family who stood by me… all the way. Also, those who genuinely love me. With them all, I could rise above my depression and anxiety and so much more while living with chronic pain.

Let me clarify that I am in no way perfect, and only God is perfect. However, I choose to do what is right before doing what is wrong. Do I sometimes fall? Absolutely, many times. I am a human being, and humans make mistakes all the time. However, for me, the desire to do what's right has always out rule doing what is wrong.

Sometimes, things in our life will go wrong, but we should never stay down from the falls.

To my readers, I will say, just learn from it and look into yourself. Peel off what needs to change for you, and live again, as the truth for me is, after trusting God with my Heart and life, but mostly now, because I am a Christian. The urge to do what is best, and mostly for other people, was a better and easier choice for me. Was I tempted? Many times, for sure. However, for me, my life was never mine to live without God. I know that now even more after my accident in twenty fifteen.

This is not about forcing anyone to change their heart. To love God the way I love him, I must say that the God I know does not force anyone to give their heart to him. All individual has to make that their choice. That was my choice and never a day have I regretted that I made serving God my choice. Now I am so happy finding me and being me for him. I was a sheltered individual, but with God's help, I now am living a powerful life, which I am now able to write about and ready to share with others.

I want to share my life because I have been through so much and believe it would be a shame to keep this life all to myself. This book is just me, talking about myself and how I can help others. The choices I make are not for everyone. Some of my family members know of the worrisome life I have lived and am still living. For those who know nothing about me and no knowledge of my life, they can now read, and I hope I can be of some help to those who have anxiety, depression, and chronic pain.

In this book, my readers will learn about some of the terrifying and horrific ordeals I have been through. Perhaps people wonder why I keep trusting God, who allows me to go through these experiences time after time. But I now understand – it is for me to help others transition from bad situations to safe and positive ones. I hope this book can also help others to understand some things we go through or have/had experienced. If we take the time to look back, living will teach us something about the way we look at life and can also help us to be stronger men and women in today's world. One that is dejected and very unpredictable.

Chapter 1
My Life At The Age Of 6 & With 5 Siblings

I remember being smart, caring, loving, and naïve. Living a sheltered life. I had loving parents and came from a large family. Mom stayed home, and Dad worked as a Jockey. Mom was loving, caring, and devoted to her family to the best she knew how. Mom was very generous to the community. She was light on punishment; however, when she did, it was from an avalanche of, stop it, or you will get it. Mom cared for my grandmother and grandfather as the remaining siblings migrated. Mom was a great cook, and everyone loved her food. Dad was great at cooking as well and would surprise us by making us fabulous meals when he had time.

My Father worked a lot and would stay at the race track more often than at home. He loved us and did the best he knew how, I believe. Dad made sure we were never hungry and were always taken care of. Dad was generous to all who knew him. However, he was very stern and ruled us with an Iron rod.

He had profoundly serious eyes. We knew the meaning of the eyes very well! Which meant to stop what we were doing, or the belt would make us stop. Dad demanded of us to have respect for elders, go to church, go to school, and do our best. However, associating with the other children in our neighborhood was not an option in my dad's book.

My parents insisted that we not play with anyone in the community or socialize with outsiders, but sometimes, my brother's broke Dad's rule after playing a football game or match. My sister and I would have father's rule in our forehead. Punishment from Dad was painful. My siblings and I were so afraid of Dad that we would try to stay out of trouble. I remember getting whoop for staying at my church friend's house later than I should have. This was rare. It was when girls as friends just wanted to talk about life, and time just moved faster with the many things we wanted to say. So that day, I forgot about my Dad's rules. My butt paid the price for forgetting.

My Dad would whoop my siblings for doing that as well. As we grew up, we did not agree with this type of punishment (with the belt); nevertheless, spanking is common in the West Indies countries. Spanking, I would say, happens due to the island's traditional way to keep their children grounded. But I would say that not all children turn out the way their family intended to spank their children. However, my siblings and I would probably say that to this day, we don't agree with the excess spanking some families inflict on their children around the world. With that said, I have come to an understanding of my Dad's perception of why he had to spank us.

I do not write this to say my Dad was an abuser. My Dad was ignorant and admitted his error when we brought it up with him later. Watching television on modern ways of disciplining and hearing about the abuse of Children from other mothers and fathers infuriated Dad, causing Dad to say, I should have done it "punishment" differently and to add that the Police should arrest people who abuse children.

Hearing Dad say the above had me convinced he had no understanding of the great effect it had on his children. Click "the light bulb in my Dad's head came on." All I could say was, good for you, Dad. I believe that Dad's anger towards our defiance in breaking his rules got the better of him. The belt kept us grounded and stopped us from crossing boundaries. We learned as we got older, and I now understand what he was trying to do.

When playing, Dad would tell us we had our siblings to play with, and that should be enough for us. We adhere to his rules, ninety-nine percent. However, Mom did associate with the community, as she was the food pantry for those who needed her help, and she continued to help when she migrated to Canada. I had no idea how effective Mom's volunteering was in the neighborhood she called home for years until she passed away. Her funeral had old and young people who came to offer their condolences and to add how Mom showed kindness to them many times while she was alive. (The community called her Mommy or Miss Vie)

My Dad approved my Mom's charity for our neighbors when we lived in Jamaica and here in Canada. Only us children were told to have only church friends and approved school friends. Dad saw things that were so bad, such as Grand Larceny, holding up people, doing drugs, and so much more.

These crimes were what some of the neighborhood children were doing.

I saw my neighbor's children holding up a guy for his sunglasses and was not able to question the action without endangering my life. I was too traumatized to bring it up, and I would not attempt to talk or mention what I saw growing up in my neighborhood. It was only after I moved to Canada that I was able to talk about it, as I was literally afraid every time I would think about it in my mind. Some of my neighbors were either in drugs, stealing, rape, and some of the most disturbing behavior that can blow the minds of anyone who want to be safe and law-abiding.

My encouragement to parents regarding what I have seen is if the environment is disturbing where your children's futures are at risk, please try very hard to see or inquire about how you can safely guard your children's future before it gets out of hand. My

Dad safeguards us in his own way, and thank God we turned out well, growing up in the hood. Just keep in mind your children can be caught up in gangs or in an endangered situation, e.g., drive-by shooting, assault, or even death. I have been through some of the above circumstances, and I thank God for his help.

My Grandmother, Grandfather, and Auntie Norma, my cousin, also laid the foundation of our good behaviors. They had a profound impact on raising us. All family members had to be polite, respectful, and possess good poise, even living in the hood. One can live in the hood and do not have to be a part of its shenanigans. Also, talking back to parents, elders, and especially to any adults and teachers, is prohibited, and if we dare to complain when we got home, we would get a whooping along with a demand to apologize to such a person.

Many parents have done their best in raising up their Children. However, some children of this era lack so much when it comes to the way they talk to their parents. I am not sure why this happens; however, I am strongly inclined that in our society, the presence of our children's friends, the neighborhood, or our environment plays a vital role in how our children behave and the future outcome of their lives, and then there are those who are so respectful, my heart melts when they speak to adults.

I commend those of you who try to be the best you can be

as you grow up, desiring to be respectful to your parents and peers and, most of all, respecting yourselves. For those who wish they could roll back the curtain to treat their family with respect, or now after reading this book, and realizing that they were not kind or respectful to people in general. I want to say that it is never too late to start or try. Just remember you can do it, and most of all, you will not regret it.

My grandparents worked hard to see their children, grandchildren, and great-grandchildren become their best selves. We all grew up in one house that had eleven rooms and two bathrooms. One for the family and another for the Tenants. We were fortunate to have a comfortable life with the basic provision that a normal family would have had at that time or era. Our comfortable lifestyle entails a roof over our heads, food on our table, clothes on our bodies, and the privilege of having our house dividing the wall of our church that had people who prayed daily for everyone.

We could climb over when we should have been in church and not at home. Having church at our doorstep was a blessing and a part of our upbringing. Everybody has different mentors in their upbringing, the above was what molded us and reshaped us into what and who we are today. I loved my grandparents, as all of us stem from the Minott family tree, and we had the best upbringing a family could have ever hoped for. Just my opinion.

However, after my grandparents died, the Minott family has never been the same. Some difficult and unpleasant disagreements about my grandparents' property have caused a rift and division among our older family members because of the money that has to be received from the property. The disagreement became nasty and shameful. However, it did not change the latter generation. I would hope that we have learned to care for family before any possessions.

The grandchildren have tried to amend the relationship by trying to stay connected. One attempt was to try and help the family get to know each other. It was a start to getting familiar with other family members that we did not know due to the estranging of the families! I believe nothing in this world should cause a family to be ripped up or be torn apart.

Family relationships are important in these challenging times. Believe me, we need each other to help us through unexpected, difficult times. My advice is to try extremely hard to work on your family relationships with your family members, and if it is impossible due to the many times you have tried to save the relationship of the family, just keep telling them that you love them. As no possessions, money or material things are worth losing our families over. Mostly, life is too short. Please don't waste it, make the best of life. I choose to have my best life living for God, who can take my life at any time.

My grandmother spoiled us. Our breakfast and dinner were prepared according to age and gender. The older ones were served first and the younger ones last.

Portion-wise, it was small as I was young. Regardless, we were always full. It was normal for our family to serve food this way. Looking back, I see the size of our bowls, from the oldest to the youngest, lying side by side on the dinner table. I remember my plate being far down the line. It took me a while to see the food on my plate. I kept looking and looking; my eyes kept moving from left to right, and my palate grew more liquefied. I remember wanting two drumsticks and only getting one, wanting more rice, but I was too small to ask for more. Not that I would not get a little more if I asked, but I had to remember that we were a big family. We had to be content with what we had on our plate.

Mama read the Bible to us often. We would sit in front of her quietly, taking in every detail as she read to us grandchildren. She taught us to love God even though we did not know the depth of her teaching when it concerned the Bible. Grannie would also tell us about the tough times in her life, as well as her life as a mother and grandmother. Those hard times had her on her knees. She had, at times, become fearful, thinking how she would feed the family.

One day stood out the most. She told us of a specific day she had no food and would put water on the stove to boil. She stood over the pot, praying in her mind while waiting for God to supply food for her family. To many of us, this seems fruitless or stupid, but we should continue to read and see how God works for those who have faith, even when the obvious (what is needed) cannot be seen. But wait for it. Then, a broad smile carved the skin around her mouth, showing her missing tooth close to the left side of her mouth and exposing the gum next to her teeth.

Mama said one day in the week, before the weekend, a lady came to the gate and asked for my grandmother, she said the lady called out, Miss Minott, Miss Minott! I am here to see Miss Minott.

Mama said when she came out to see who was calling for her, the lady at the gate told Mama that God told her, mama needed food to feed her family and she brought what was in her hands to feed the family. She had provisions of many kinds and can food for meat. (My mother concurred). We were incredibly happy and shockingly amazed at what my grandmother shared with us.

Back then in my grandmother's time, people talked of similar experiences related to my grandmother's, and hearing other telling so many stories that had me convinced that people trusted God before and during my grandmother's time. So, even if my mother didn't concur, I still would believe it because we have heard others talking about similar encounters. This is not only true in Jamaica but in other countries as well. So, I believed my grandmother as she had no reason to lie to us.

Every time I remember her story, and especially when I am faced with difficulties, I would get down on my knees and pray for Gods' help, and the spirit of God would either whisper to my mind to Wait, Yes or No. Most of the time, I couldn't understand it. However, over time, I got to understand why I got the answer I got at the time. All I can say is WOW! "Relating to my grandmother's story" That's what I call Faith.

Grandma also told us that she was paralyzed and was not able to walk for a while, which hindered her again to care for her family. She would pray for God to heal her, but at times, it was to no avail. Mama was not getting better. However, one day she said, she heard a Voice in her head telling her to stand up. She had not had any feelings in her legs for a long time. However, she muscled up the strength to stand and was joyfully surprised she could standup.

Grandma told us that she began to walk and kept walking slowly, and slowly until she got to the entrance of her bedroom door which was close to our passage. (Hall way) She stood at the door for a while, just hoping someone would see her. While she was standing, my Mom saw my grandma standing there.

Shocked and bewildered, Mom holler to her, "my Mom yelled, come, mama is walking."

"Mama is walking again." (The story mama told us was concurs by my mother as well.) I remember we all smiled, as we were so happy for our grandmother.

Mama was a woman who loved God. She had integrity and was known to place her trust in God always.

She relied on the power of a Sovereign God whom she believed in. We, her grandchildren and her children, all followed her footsteps. She had set an example for us to follow. Yes, we trust in God for our every need. Our faith has been tried many times; nevertheless, we stand firm in our belief in God, and I know, God knows I do, with all my heart. I believe most of our family does too. I say sadly, however, not all of our family has such strong belief in God for their every needs.

Every holiday, especially Christmas and Easter, we experience pure Joy and happiness. To this day, emotions still run through my mind, as I am reminiscing about my past life. Even writing this book, I can feel the warm feeling shower through my body. The feelings that I had and felt with my family at those times were the best. Those days were jovial, fun, and funny, and we enjoyed those, Moments. If any of us was hurting, we all felt hurt.

We fought with each other, yet we stuck with each other. We critiqued each other, and we comforted each other. We cry together; we celebrate with each other. We were so close. It was so wonderful to have a bonded family when my grandmother was alive. What changed as we all grew up? Keep reading to find out.

After talking with my brother, he reminded me that we all went to school at the church next door to us. At that time, I was three years old. From age four to six, we all went to Miss Burke school (kindergarten), then onto Providence Primary and Briefly to Papine Secondary, and for four years to Merl Grove High School, where I graduated with CXCs and O levels, then went on to better days.

My siblings and I played many games that I believe were played by many generations to generations all over the world. To name a few, dandy shanty, hide and seek (hiding an object for someone to find and calling out you are hot, you are cold), and another is ringing a ring a rosy. Doctors and patients, teacher and students, volleyball, basketball, netball, cricket (a West Indies sport), table tennis, and so many more.

Before school, we (my brothers and sisters) had to get up exceedingly early to run over the stadium in Jamaica on an outdoor track before we went to school. We would then shower, eat, and got ready for school. Dad would sometimes drive us to school when he had a car, but most of the time, we would take the bus. Taking the bus felt like being in a packed chicken coop. The collector and one or two passengers or I would be hanging outside the door, holding tight onto a rail within the bus as the bus drove extremely fast. That was very scary for on the moving bus.

However, to exit (crazy but true), the passenger who needs to exit the bus or to exit a taxi car would shout "One-stop driver," and the driver would stop for that person to get off. The crazy thing is that the bus conductor would take on more passengers than what they dropped off, even when the bus is packed to its max. If you do not have a car, you would dread every day to rely on the bus. That was when Jamaica was my primary home. I would imagine it is the same or worse and hoping it will get better or has gotten better.

Back to Dad. Dad would make us drink bitter medicine the week before the first semester of each new school year oh...how we hated those Moments (I do not remember the name of it. however, it was so, so bitter!) I hated the beginning of school every year for that reason. Dad got angry at my older and younger brothers for their unruly (rare) behavior of not doing their chores and sometimes not following his demands. Dad would want to spank us, but we would use our house cellar to hide from Dad or our grandmother's room, which was the best place to hide. (Dad would never go into my grandmother's room). My Dad respected my grandmother. At times, I thought he was afraid of her. To tell the truth, it was not fear but a genuine respect for her.

On special days for dinner, Dad would see to it that Mom prepared the beans for dinner that was so bitter it was hard to digest due to its bitter taste. We would sit in a circle and pretend to eat the bean, using a hole in the floor that was conveniently there for us to discard the beans through the floor opening, giving us the opportunity yet again, to put our taste buds out of misery. One day, Dad and Mom noticed that something was growing through the hole in the floor.

Noticing the small tree and looking like the plant of the bitter bean evolving through the floor. Dad said to Mom, that look like a small susuba tree "vie" (my Dad's pet name for my Mom). He firmly told Mom to watch us after that day onward.

Mom and Dad would watch us after then, just to make sure we ate the beans. Oh!! Our lives were miserable from then. We had to eat the beans whether we liked it or not. The green beans were selected to clean our blood along with another herb. (Dad said that our body needed the nutrients from the beans as well as to clean our blood.) We didn't care, as it was not pleasant to our taste buds.

After the reveal, we had to eat the bitter beans more often than we wanted to, as Dad's eyes and belt had us in fear. I am sure many people like beans and enjoy them as well. Great for them! We, my siblings and I loathe the beans, no matter how many ways it has been prepared. I vowed that I would never eat that beans when I leave to be on my own and to this day, I kept the promise I made at my young age.

Now, being older, we can laugh about things of that nature when reminiscing about the past. Some days, my third oldest brother and I would sometimes steal food out of the pot and deny we did that. Mom caught my brother and reprimanded him. Me seeing how angry my mom was with my brother made me stop stealing out of the pot. I overheard her telling him he was not going to get any meat with his food, and I did not want to hear that, as I also love having a little meat on my bones. This is ironic as I'm now not a lover of meat but a love of the marrow from within the bones. Some people think I am very weird to love bone marrow when it takes so much effort to get to it.

At the age of seven/eight, my grandmother sent me to the supermarket to get something she needed to make dinner. We usually were sent to the store mostly, on a day or second day, to get grocery for dinner. The store manager knew my grandmother, and my grannie made a list for me to give the store manager every time we went shopping. That day, at the store, a man came up to me while I was standing in line and told me that my grandmother wanted me to follow him to his house so he could give me something for her. I didn't know the man, but my grandmother knew a lot of people, and being young and naïve, I got out of the line and followed the man, walking as the man rode on his bicycle beside me.

Knowing what I know now, I would never have done what I did then. I remember the man stopping and getting off his bike, asking me for the money that my grandmother gave me to buy the groceries so that he could secure it tightly. I saw the man taking the money and folding it, securing the money inside, and even making two ties, one at each end.

What the man told me to tell my grandmother was that he would deliver what he wanted to give her at our house later on that day. (What was it? that he was supposed to give me to give to my grandma, but I don't remember at this Moment.) What I remember is that I had to run back to the supermarket as it was such a long walk back to the supermarket since I left to get groceries.

When I got to the store and was ready to pay for the groceries, there was no money in the handkerchief, which was tied so firmly. I said out loud, oh no "him Tek the money" (meaning I was scammed!) Tears began to roll down my face. I slowly walked home, which felt like forever, as I was not sure what I was going to tell my grandmother. The grocery owner did not give me the groceries because I had no money to pay for it.

When I was near my house, I cried even more, as my grandmother could not afford to lose her money. My grandmother reared pigs, chickens, ducks and used the proceeds to buy her groceries for the family. It is still heartbreaking to remember that incident, even though it was so long ago.

At the time, I was thinking then that we would starve as there was no money to buy food. Anyway, when I got home and told my grandmother what had happened, she was so kind and caring. She told me she did not know the man and asked if he touched me, and I told her no. He only took the money. Grandma then told me never to do that again as he could have harmed me.

The lesson with the scammer taught me many things along my journey, and believe me, I have had many close call encounters with men who were evil. One followed me, driving slowly (in a normal situation, I may have never notice that someone on foot or by car is following me), but thanks to God for allowing me to go through the earlier ordeal at a young age, that prepared and guided me, and alarm me that I would probably have died already. I now know it was a lesson for my future.

I can now say thanks to God for allowing me to go through that lesson without harm to help others and myself for those future crises later in my life. I met men who I did not know, wanting to give me a ride to where I was going. Some of those men's eyes screamed evil when they stopped to give me a ride. Their eyes led me to believe they were predators, and if I didn't have that early experience, I probably would have taken rides from some of those men.

Later on in my book, I will talk more about one or two fearful encounters with an evil spirit, which was another frightening Moment in my life. I had to trust God more than I ever did, as my life depended on how much I believed God. As he saw me through those encounters back then. The need to cry out to God at that Moment was imminent. My body had no choice then but to freeze for a few seconds, which seemed like a long time. I now understand that that was what it meant to have faith in God. (Hebrews 11: 1)

Chapter 2

Describing My Siblings and I

At a young age before year fifteen, I shared my life with six siblings. We are born with different characters, behaviors, and abilities. My oldest brother who is now deceased. He was a very smart guy who was an accountant. However, he was a disciplinarian.

He would, at times, take on the characteristics like my Dad. Disciplining us when we did anything wrong.

Sadly, sometimes, he uses the belt buckle to discipline us the younger siblings. He did not know better at that time. Anyways, he learned differently as he got older. He was the one helping us with our homework every day. I remember him doing my homework for me when the subject was hard and telling me to look it over until I figured it out. Sometimes, I did figure it out, and sometimes I did not.

There were times when I took the work he did and forgot to rewrite it over in my hand writing and was severely punished by my teacher with the belt, and learned not to do that again. From then my teacher would always call on me to make sure that I did the work for myself. Of course, I had to, as it was a painful lesson to carry for the years ahead. (Those were the days when teachers were allowed to use the belts on children) I am thankful that does not happen anymore to children of this age.

My second oldest brother lives here in Canada. He loves animals and has a collage of them. He had rabbits, birds of varied species, and pigeons. He was serious and loved to play and coach football (soccer) under seventeen teams. When we were younger, I remember after my sister left for Canada, he and I shared a room.

My bed was closer to the wall, "don't forget we lived in the hood," and he was closer to the entrance of the door. During those days, it was okay to sleep in the same room with my siblings. My brother and I spent hours late into the night, talking and laughing about many things.

My sister, who followed next, was smart and a survivor of Breast Cancer. She loves to dress in the finest apparel. She had to always look the best, even to this day, no matter where we were going. She would stand out in the crowd. She even won the neighborhood pageant, and yes, I came second. She was the one who sponsor us all here in Canada. If I never say thanks. I would like to say to her this Moment when she reads this book. Thanks, Yvonne, for caring and helping us experience living in one of the most beautiful countries in the world.

My next brother was the hilarious one. He is very, very funny. He would give us an alias that stuck with us even to this day. I will not mention the names in my book, but I will say I hated my alias and refuse to answer when anyone calls me by my alias. I would tell them that I left that name back in Jamaica. Other children call me "Redhead Gal." Some of my family members hated their alias as well; I know my sister hated hers. Others did not care.

My brother could tell the best of jokes that had stomachs hurting for a long time. Friends and family enjoyed his jokes, especially the one about when he snatched my sister's pudding from her hand. I will disclose this one. One day, I remember my sister eating a pudding called blue draws, (maybe called another name in other west indies countries, with the same recipe.) I do not know where they got these names for food, but yes, that was the name of the pudding. My brother grabbed the pudding out of her hand and ran through our gate to the road outside.

I remember seeing my sister taking up a stone and throwing it over our wall. I do not think he got to finish eating the pudding as (I must laugh at this Moment) my brother came running through the gate crying that someone busted open his head, and he was not sure who did it. We all laugh hysterically. We laughed aloud and said good….it will stop you from stealing people's food from their hands. This was a regular thing done by my brother. He learned from that day to ask for some of our food instead of grabbing food out of our hands or from our plates. See what I mean, all stages in our life journey help to mold us for the good times in life, or some of us will never learn and will pay sadly for the worst in life's journey.

Reminiscing at this Moment, we would play a game to see who would laugh first, and when it was my brothers' turn to tell jokes, we had to brace ourselves to stay put in this game, or we would be out sooner than we wanted. I was closer to him than the rest of my siblings as we were born the same month, a year apart, and shared many fun Moments when I lived in Jamaica. He was into dating multiple girls, and I was worried about that. He always tells me he is ok.

Now, I worry less as he is now focusing on getting his daughter through high school and onto higher learning. My brother has so many children that I always worry about him not having the means to take care of them. To men out there who think it is cool to countless women and sleep with them, I would like to say it is not cool. It's actually selfish and senseless. Your children are the ones who usually suffer the consequences of your bad decisions and sometimes carry it through their relationships.

My sister Carol lives in Jamaica, she is strong-willed and adventurous. We all got along well. However, I do not have any memories of Carol as we grew older. She went to live with her grandmother.

She was my Dad's child. We extended our love and welcomed her. The time we spent together had it's up and down. However, I still remember her throughout my life and am still in touch with her today. We WhatsApp each other now and then, and I am happy even if that all we both can do to stay connected.

My youngest brother is no longer here with us as well. My heart breaks every time I think about him and more so much as I write about him. He was the youngest but behaved like the oldest. He had the traits of growing up too fast. Delano changed when he joined the Jamaican Army. Sometimes, he would want to tell us what to do and would be upset or unhappy with us when we reminded him and was the youngest. He and I sometimes verbally and physically fight a lot, verbally as all siblings occasionally do.

However, he and I did a little more than fighting verbally. We would be throwing objects at each other, sometime even throwing stones at each other when we had disagreements. I remember he and I saying mean things to each other as well. We both knew no better at the time. We were young and silly. Yet the next day, we were once again brother and sister. We had no malice among us growing up. The love remained true. We both knew no better. However, we grew out of our childish behaviors and habits. It simply means we have grown up and now know better.

In my youngest brother's mind, he knew it all and wanted to prove it to all of us. Delano knew he was my mom's best child. He and my oldest brother. Just my opinion. However, Mom said she loved us equally and had no favorite. It did not bother me. I knew Mom and Dad loved us all in their own way.

Delano got away with many things, and we, his siblings, were not happy about the above, and at times, we would take our anger out on him. He would tough it out most of the time when we got back at him. I remember also him punching me in the pit of my stomach for agreeing with my older brothers in a disagreement they all had one day. His playing was rough at times. Yet he didn't mean to… when any of us got hurt.

Another day we all were playing together, covering each other under a sheet. My siblings had me under the cover (for a very long time or what I believe was a very long time). I could not breath. I was screaming and kicking and crying. No one was hearing me when I was screaming for my siblings to let me out from under the cover. I had to pinched Delano very hard as he was the one saying, "don't let her out, don't let her out, and more.

After I was able to get from under the cover, I was then able to breath. I screamed at him, letting him know that he almost suffocated me. He was the one who was loudly saying the above "hold her down, hold her down, do not take the cover off her".

We were just playing, which was ok. However, sometimes we tend to overdo things, and then an accident happens. I say this to let my readers know that when playing, please remember to listen to the person who is in danger and act on the plea and do what should be done in a life-taking moment. He told me he was very sorry and that he never meant to try to suffocate me. I told him it was a horrifying experience. Playing is fun, that is why it's called playing. However, it can lead to a catastrophic scenario.

Another day we were playing a game of passing a rock around, trying to move our hand quickly so that we would not have our fingers crushed by the rock; the game had five people sitting in a circle. Thinking now about that game, it was a stupid game to play. To continue, everyone was moving the rock around fast, and all of us had to quickly move around the stone so we would not smash the other with the rock. Then, as we move faster and as the game got more intense, we decided to stop. Anyway, I remember at the end of the game my right hand was still on the ground, and Delano picked- up the rock and slammed it down on my big finger literally, taking it off and immediate spuing blood all over us.

I went into shock, seeing my finger being held up by the skin. I then heard Delano screaming, "Oh no! I'm sorry, I'm so sorry". I did not mean to do that. I don't even know or remember what I said to him. All I can remember was a lady in our house (living as a tenant in our house) running for something she called

"Blue Stone", (in Jamaica) I did not know what it was for, all I knew at the time was the lady running to her room to get it, as she said it would heal my finger very fast.

After the incident, the lady made it her duty to care for my finger. It healed. The lady was right, as it was fully healed after a few weeks, and I did not have to go to the hospital to have the finger stitched up. I carried no hard feeling for Delano. I was always on high alert when playing with him. Why talking about my youngest brother more than the others? His life was interesting. I will continue to talk about him some more.

My grandmother sheltered Delano from my dad's whopping many times when he did anything wrong. Mom and Mama stepped in many times when Dad needed to discipline him with the belt. Because he was the youngest, it hurt them both, they said. They hated to see him being punished with the belt. My dad was brutal with the belt, and we all feared him. Delano had birthdays up to the age of twelve when his older siblings, including myself had not even one. Are we bitter? No, we were many. So, all of us had to celebrate our birthday on his day collectively with him, as our parents could not afford to have a party for each of their children. Let me say we understood. I hope my siblings felt the same way I did. If not, I am speaking for myself.

Delano had a gift and was very, very talented at playing football. He could have had a chance to play professional football (What we call soccer here in Canada) and let it pass by because he did not want to practice but wanted to play. He believed he was so good and should not have to practice the sport when the team was practicing. To tell the truth, he was really…. really good, but no one who plays any type of sports is beyond rehearsing or practicing with their fellow teammates. All my brothers played football; however, he was the best at the game.

Amidst all this, I loved him and even when he is no longer here, my love is still strong for my younger brother. We were not on speaking terms at the time of his death. I was sad about it all. My youngest brother was not only speaking to me, but he was not speaking to my other siblings as well. Still, a part of me sank and, truthfully, has not been put to rest to this day.

The how! What? Why? with his passing? I am still working on as the feelings I now harbor due to the way he died; I would like to let it lie to console my memory of pain. Therefore, I leave it to God as God is the only one who knows what happened why he was shot by the police. That said, I refuse to judge, and I will leave it there. I truly love and miss him. I have many good memories and I choose to focus on those good times we had together. Now to talk about me.

I remember being a strong-willed child and having a soft side to me as well. However, it did not stop a girl in grade school from bullying me. I did not know what to do but to cry and complain to my mom all the time, and did not want to go to school because of the bulling. My mom told me to report the bullying or defend myself. I was only four or five at the time in kindergarten. I remember even to this day, that I personally would take as much as I could until someone tries to break me. It was then, and only then, I would let whomever was getting the best of me, to know how sad and hurtful they were to me.

The strong-will side of me back then as a kindergarten came out as I remembered what my mom said but did nothing about it when I went to school that day.

Three days later, the bully again continued to slap me in the head. I remember what my mom told me and what happen, is that, I pushed the bully down on the ground when she came up in my face to push and slap me. Doing that frightened moment, she backed off and went crying. I believe I defend myself without doing great harm and have learnt how to help myself and others. I would not then and would not now encourage anyone to take matters into their own hands. However, telling the teacher, the principal, your parents or someone is a smart thing to do.

Bullying others should not be accepted.

As I got older, I learned to restrain myself mentally, emotionally, and physically. However, I must admit that I gave my grandmother challenging moments in raising me. I do not remember if any of my siblings gave my grandparents challenges. However, I remember being mouthy and having an answer for everything. I remember trying very hard to please others before pleasing myself. A trait I became and kept as I grew older. I grew up letting people walk all over me as I have a soft heart even to this day.

Chapter 3

A Glimpse Into Six To Thirteen-Year-Old Me

Let me recall my grade school years. I remember getting up in the mornings with all my siblings from the touch of my mom's hand and the chattering of my brothers and sisters when she woke us up. Dad was waiting for us to start our exercise for the morning as usual. We had to go over the stadium not too far from us, to run around the track for an hour. Can you imagine? Dad believed children should get sleep, and exercise (running the stadium track) each morning, followed by a shower before having our breakfast, which was porridge. The selection was my mom's choice or just what she had at home for that day. Each day was either (Cornmeal, oatmeal, banana, or rice Porridge) with a slice of bread to dip in it. After our morning run, we the young ones would get tire easy and want to stop, but Dad's eyes were watching, so we had to tough it up. After all that, we were driven or took the bus to school. I did well at Grade School and had so much fun.

I remember we would be in class, learning all we should, to prepare us for High school. That was when my teacher taught me what the word "sex" on a test meant. I guess I wasn't paying attention in grade school. Thank God. As I would be so embarrassed learning the above in high school. When I was eight going on nine, I believed my schoolteacher shunned me, causing me to be very sad that I did not want to go to school.

At the time, I believed that she, the teacher, was showing favoritism to students and, on top of it all, hated me. I untangle the above problem by opening up to my mom. My mom came to my school and talked to my teacher about my feelings of not wanting to attend school. I know there is someone out there who can resonate with what I was experiencing at that tender age. (a misunderstanding between the teacher and the teacher towards you.)

The teacher told my mom that I was a child who raised my hand for many questions, and she just wanted other students to get the chance to raise their hands as well and that she needed to give other children the chance to be chosen instead of choosing me. I did not understand why that was at the time, but as I grew older, I appreciated the teacher even more than anyone in the class. (Only my opinion) The teacher did not take my accusation personally. From then in grade school, I learned that all things are not as they seem. I remember my teacher shaking my hand and saying to me. "Claudia, thanks for standing up for yourself". I remember those words even today.

My takeaway from that experience was that I should have gone to the teacher so she could explain why she called on other children when my hand was raised first before the others. (Anyway, it's good to find out the real reason, especially when it has to do with judging others.) Maybe I didn't want to speak up because I was fearful of other children resenting me.

I now know that others may not like us if we voice our opinions in the classroom, at work or other events.

Nonetheless, keep standing up for yourself. Just take courage and always be a leader and not a follower.

Friends and people's words come and go all the time. You may even feel sad at times over some of our end results in school or anywhere where others are voicing their opinions. Don't feel sad as those friends or people may not be the right friends for you or me. (I now know, having experienced many bad outcomes.) However, if the situation doesn't allow you to assert those traits in you, just be yourself and really, that's all you need to do in life. (For me, God is all I need in my life when peoples and life fails me.)

I grew up after that. I wasn't ruffled, knowing my parents' demand for us not to play with anyone in the community. I felt safe and empowered to be independent as I grew older. I was one along with some of my siblings, who stood out in many things or almost everything we did, even to this day. I remember I would sit between my mother's or grandmother's legs as they would comb my hair. I had reddish-to-brown kinky hair. I would scream and hallow as hard as I could.

My siblings would all laugh at me when it was my turn, Jeering me. My mom would say to me, (Shut Yu mouth, Yu too nasty) (Canadians would say, Quiet, stop being nasty.) Saying I should have gotten accustomed to combing my hair by now. Believe me, it was like standing in a - 50-degree winter storm, yelling for the bus to come so I could get out of the cold, especially after my mom washed my hair.

At six, going on seven, I remember Dad telling my oldest brother that he would oversee the young ones and that he should make sure we did our homework and chores around the house. One day, my dad asked my eldest brother to ensure the water bottles had water in the fridge, which my brother usually does see to it we do, but on a particular day, my eldest brother could not fill the water bottle, so my eldest brother asked my younger brothers to fill the water bottles and to make bags of juice, so that all the children including himself, could have something to drink when we needed to.

When my brother got home, he realized that my younger brothers forgot to do what he asked, knowing that my younger brothers forgot, they ran and went hiding from my oldest brother. My eldest brother was yelling that he got home late from studying at school and was thirsty and needed a bag of juice to drink, and if dad found out there was no juice, he would be the one in trouble. Not able to find my brothers, my oldest brother told me to fill the water bottles, so I did.

On returning, I fell and cut open my right hand and cut open my veins, causing me to get thirty-nine stitches to close the opening on my right hand. I remember running everywhere as I was in shock, seeing my hand bleeding everywhere, and did not know what to do. I remember Auntie Norma getting a hold of me and looking for something to tie the upper part of my hand, I did not know why at that moment, as I was in shock, seeing so much blood.

Now I know I almost died; that's why the moment was chaotic and dire.

My brother or Aunty Norma, one or both, putting me on their back and running with me to the Children's Hospital. Thank God, it was walking distance away from where we lived. I remembered the Doctors and nurses working on me, and then I was out until I heard someone saying she was sleeping so peacefully. I also heard someone calling my name over and over again. I did not understand what the Doctor or the Nurses did to me at the time, but now I know. They were trying to save my life.

My dad punished my brother for putting me in such a predicament. Life was difficult, as I was not able to do my chores because I was right-handed. However, at that age, everyone was doing my chores, and was at my advantage. It was a joyful time, as I was living as a queen with my siblings catering to me. I remember smiling all the time for six months. I have the scar to remind me of that dreadful day and treated like a queen.

At the age of eight plus, I had challenges, and some unusual and weird things happened to me. I remember my dad not being home for a week as he was working. I was coming from my school friend's house when I noticed a figure walking behind me with no head. I was curious and was wondering why he was following me. I started quickening my pace. I turned to open the gate of my house and a few steps after, I noticed the figure turning and walking through my gate, without opening it.

It was then I started to panic as I was thinking what is this? And why was the figure still behind me? I was about to call out for my mom when the spirit of God within me said don't say a word, just keep walking.

Honestly, I continued to walk towards my bedroom door that I shared with my siblings back then, not looking back as I was shaking like the breeze blowing leaves from left to right and back and forth. I kept walking through my passage and turned the doorknob to enter my bedroom and into bed. I slid under the sheet quickly without changing my clothes or brushing my teeth. It was at that time that I felt a presence over me and saw the scariest thing.

Just imagine the figure was standing over you. I could feel the piercing presence and wanted to call out to my mother and dad, but it was then a still calm voice inside my head saying to me, you don't want to do that. (And I quote, the thoughts at the time plain as I said it above) Then, after a brief second, the figure turned around and walked through my door again without anyone hearing it opening.

The above is the truth and make me quiver as I write this part. I knew at that moment it was an evil spirit that followed me into my house and in my bedroom. Remembering that, I wanted to scream but kept calm. I prayed and eventually fell asleep. The next morning, I told my mom, and she told me it was a good thing that I did not say anything as it could have hurt me as the evil spirit that hurt my sister when we were in primary school. (Grade School)

Why did my mom say that to me? I knew then, and I will now tell you the true story of my sister's encounter with an evil spirit being. We went to school on a good day. Nothing was wrong, only that our school ground where we played with other students was in a huge graveyard and we played around the tomb everyday back then and nothing went wrong and nothing was unusual. We played skipping with a rope and ran around the tombs, which we did every day during recess. Except on that day!

On that day, my sister and her friends were skipping with a rope when my sister just fell to the ground and started foaming from her mouth. My sister's eyes rolled around in the socket of her head. She was behaving differently, and we, my brothers, myself, my friends, and frighten student, the principal, and the teacher, could not figure out what had and was happened to my sister. We took her home and placed her on the bed as we did not know what was happening and why she was just jumping on the bed and screaming that the man was in the room with her. During that time, we did not see who or whom she was pointing at. But I guess I was too young and did not know what was happening at the time. It was weird.

I thought I could see every Ghostly figure, and believe me, I did sometimes. I, however, saw nothing that day. We all were looking around the room. Some of the elders, church pastor and members said they saw the figure my sister was seeing. The only thing I could add was that God did not want me to see that bad energy (evil spirit) at that moment. However, there was an evil, airy sense of a presence in our midst that I could feel but not see. I knew something was wrong, but I did not know what my mom and dad could do? It's not that we could take her to the Doctor as she was not physically sick, but her behavior was calling for a Pastor. (what some people called a Priest) to pray for her as we were dealing with something we could not see. (A bad energy/evil spirit).

My sister was always jumpy and screaming for two days, and the socket of her eyeball was constantly rolling over. (We, West Indies born, was familiar with evil spirits walking around as if they were still alive.) I do not expect people who have never experienced evil around them to understand what I am writing in this book; however, all my brothers, mom, dad, church friends, and maybe a few neighbors knew what had happened to my sister and could relate and understood what Yvonne was going through.

No doctors could help/fix my sister's issue. Only God could. She got better with many prayers and healing from God. (This is a true event that happened to my sister). I just thought I would share this with those who could understand. I know those who haven't and cannot understand will take issue to what I am saying; however, be thankful God allowed you all not to see or experience what I am saying. Perhaps you would freak out. Sorry, but I have to tell the next encounter. Please bear with me to tell just one more. If this is too much for any of my readers, you can turn to the next page.

The next encounter with an evil spirit on another day was when I was walking in my passage in Jamaica when I tried to opened the door to my mother's room. I felt a strange, airy feeling on the other side of the door. My head starts feeling weird, like the presence of an evil being. I tried to scream but no one was hearing me, "just picture you having a scary dream after watching a scary movie." After you awoke from that dream, you were still shaking, but you were okay--as it was just a dream.

Mine didn't end like that. Remember how you felt at the time? Well, I still get the quiver every time I remember the experience. I tried to open the door, but it could not open. It was then I heard my grandmother reprimanding what was on the other end of the door. Grandma was Grandma was walking up and down our passage, telling the evil spirit to leave our home and go back to where it came from. While she was walking up and down, I tried another time to open the door and it did open after she raised her voice even higher.

I ran to my grandmother, and she held me close to her, and she said to me (and I quote: My child, you do not have to say anything. I know what happened a minute ago. You do not have to tell me.) I was comforted as my grandmother knew, and I did not have to explain. People before my time and around my age had those unsettling and scary things happening to them. You would think we were in a scary movie, and the spirits were testing us. I know it still happens in some countries all over the world. e.g.

'Haiti' Nevertheless, I try to forget those days now that I am in another Country. It's still hard to explain to those who never and would never understand. There are so many other encounters, but I will leave it where I can tell you of the ones I remember at this point.

It was another morning. Dad was home. Before school, Dad once again ensured we began our usual routine-running around the track for an hour, half-asleep and dragging our feet. His watchful eyes followed our every move, making sure we didn't take shortcuts. We were young and tired, desperate to stop, but his silent presence pushed us to keep going. Looking back, it was a life shaped by discipline and early morning workouts-something we never chose, yet had no voice to refuse.

Chapter 4
In My Own Words Age 17

Started High School, the Principal, and the home-room teacher would explain all the cons and pros of starting high school. Thank God for a friend who gave me the jump-start. I hope she will read my book, as I would like to say thank you my friend.

I presume it would be a lot of work, as high school was the start of figuring out how and what I wanted to do going forward into the adult stage of my life. To be honest, I did not know at the start of my high school year what I wanted to be. My brain was confused and underdeveloped at that age, and I had to take a long look inside me, close to fourth form, to see where I fit in. Going to high school was surreal. The experience is one I will never forget. I had the most amazing time and am now ready to share. I started high school at the age of fourteen and was ready for the experience. I got up once again from the touch of my mom's hand and sometimes from the chattering of my brothers.

I maintain a reserved demeanor in high school, preferring a small circle of friends. While not the top performer academically, I took my studies seriously and valued those who shared the same mindset. (with the exception of my Spanish class) as no one can get those days back. High school is important, so don't waste it having fun without thinking about the future. I say this to let others know that what you put in is what you receive, and I will add that you should never cheat yourself to get to where you see yourself in the years to come. Take advantage of the opportunity while you can. It's important for the journey ahead.

The first day I had my English class, it was okay. My teacher was a lecturer, and I was uneasy in her class and wondered if it was my teacher or me. Anyways, I eventually loved English. An hour later was accounting. I loved accounting and enjoyed going to class every day. I was one of those students who were at the top of my class in accounting and could not wait for the next day to have another class.

Religious Studies was also on the same day, and it was just okay as I was not hearing what I was taught at my church. The studies were different, so I didn't do as well as some of my friends expected. I got a pass. Still, it was not a big deal as I was not studying religion as a career.

History was good, and I did well in class. I was not sure what I was going to do with a history class at the end of high school. It was mandatory, and I had to give it the best I could, and I did. I had science class, and my teacher at that time took me aside and told me one day not to make nursing my career as my experiments were always wrong or blowing up. At this moment,

I have to chuckle as it is now ironic that I graduated with honors in the medical office administration program at Durham College.

Can you imagine if I had ignored what my teacher said when I was young? I could have been a strong contender and could have become a nurse if I tried hard with some encouragement or as an accountant which were two of my choices after leaving High school. My finances were tight, so going to university could not take president. Due to the challenges of financial independence deterred me from getting further into higher education at that time. A Nursing career was off the table as well. (No thanks to one of my high school teachers)

After leaving the USA, I was so worried about continuing my studies in Canada. (I completed one semester of University Courses towards the accounting program and got a letter advising me to Matriculate at the time, but I couldn't, I was leaving for Canada). As I would have to take on a costly program that I couldn't afford, and I didn't want to asked my parents knowing they just got to Canada or to asked my sister as she had her own expenses. The cost to help me to register was high and I couldn't do it to anyone nor myself. I just didn't have the money. Nonetheless, I took the recommendation of my teacher and believed I would not do well in science. I was still young and thought I would do something that was just as good when it comes to making ok money. Also, the reason I am telling this story is to help or give others my experience in high school and for them to listen to your own instinct.

Your teacher's suggestions, other student's advice or any sort of advice that you received should not deter you from your choice and your decision when it concerns your studies now or in the future. Listing to your Parents, family members, teacher, or friends is still ok. However, the final choice to make would be yours and your capability and determination to see it through. (This is for those who will read my book and say this sounds like a piece of good advice if they are going through the same or similar experience as they come to a decision). Never let anyone tell you that you cannot succeed in life or, your choice in career. Your choice is yours and yours only to succeed. Make sure you do something that you love and that you will succeed at. That's what matters as a whole.

In Spanish class, the teachers' way of lecturing us at the beginning of the class was about the birds and the bees. I felt that, I got enough lectures from my strict dad and did not need another from my Spanish teacher. Yet, I did not behave unseemly. Spanish class was hard and a classmate of mine at the time shared the same feeling that I felt, and we goofed off together. I am ashamed to say this, but when I had a Spanish test, I would re-write the same Spanish question in the space below the questions, and what made me feel okay doing the above was that I had my friend who followed suit as well. The teacher would give me a lecture after placing the biggest 0/100. Was I concerned? Absolutely, my mom and dad were going to give me a whooping, probably a hard lesson to bare.

However, I hoped I could let them understand that I just couldn't understand Spanish.

Did I regret not giving Spanish a chance? Absolutely! But at the time, I wasn't thinking, and being young added to the goofing off. I now know that having a second language is beneficial in the world and can give us more opportunities in life. Never forget the youth of this era. Speaking the language would have been beneficial as I was attracted to a few Spanish-speaking guys and also had some Spanish-speaking friends, and I would have loved to engage in a dialogue with them. Were the friends, marriage material? I don't know, as I was too afraid and shy to engage with any of them.

At the time, I knew I would be moving to Canada soon and did not know, what benefits I could offer to any of them. A lot of people know that Canada is very cold and probably would think twice to move to Canada if they knew I was moving there. However, I hoped you my readers, will see; how important it is to have a second language if the opportunity was given to you. This is just another encouragement to all of you.

Then it was my favorite, math! I loved math and was always happy to sit in my math class. Math was a hard subject and it took lots of practice to concur the dreaded subject for many, even to this day. I felt bad when I didn't do well on some of my math tests back- in the days. However, Overall, I've always tried to do my best, but when the test was hard, I consoled myself with an affirmation that It was ok to get a lower grade sometimes, but I would try to do better next time. Back then, I wish I had parents who were educated and could have helped us along the way. If you my readers, do, be thankful and take the help that's extended to you in any way or form.

Mom and Dad knew the basics in addition and subtraction, and with that, you could not fool them when it came to money. Not studying in school was unacceptable to them. Knowing that my oldest brother was assigned to help us. Eventually, my brother got a job overseas to work for the government of Jamaica in Ottawa, Canada, and therefore, our tutoring brother was no longer available to help us with our home-work. Not good for us but good for my eldest brother. He lived in New York City and died in 2023.

My brothers and I had to do the studying on our own. High school years were tough without him. However, it was what we made it to be that counted. I loved the journey as I surrounded myself with great friends who wanted each other to succeed. I graduated high school, feeling proud of myself as I was the one to give the speech for my class at the end of our school year.

We were all proud of each other and wished each other the best that life had to offer for the years ahead. I was not fortunate to have a graduation ball or a celebration, as my Parents could not afford to buy me a graduation dress at that time and after telling my cousin (who I called Aunty Norma), who lived in Canada at the time. She sent me the prettiest blue dress I have ever seen.

I am very thankful for whatever I had then. Sorry, but during my time, none of my friends had a cell phone. They had cameras, but I did not want to asked them to take a picture of me, as I was not sure when I would see any of them again. My encouragement to those who one day would read my book or share it with a family or a friend is, there are people in our circle who can help us with classes that are beyond our learning ability. Please don't be timid to seek help as we live in a society and in many countries where help is now readily available and accessible.

Just never choose the path that leads to disaster, yielding in the wrong way can cause emotional pain and disappointment in life. Most of all, do not waste your parents' money, as they try very hard, working tirelessly, to give you a better life. Some of your parents cannot even afford to send you to get a higher learning. Most of the time, especially when we come from the more impoverished areas of the state or province we live in. Also, an opportunity they never had.

Formulate your goals and your aspiration, and try your best at whatever you're good at. Just know you got it.

A purpose God has mapped out for you that you have to search your inner self for. Take on your life's journey, which is a head waiting for you, and with that, run with it. Let me appeal to you all. Never follow others on the wrong path, as it can keep you from a great career or a great life you could have had. But I must say in my book to you is having God in your life will be the best source to produce the best outcome for your life.

No pressure, but think about it and try God and see how your life turns out. One thing I will say is that life, with God or without God, does come with trials and disappointments. The best of it all is that God promises in his word that he will never leave you or forsake you, while you are going through your difficulties or in the trials you face when they arrive.

Chapter 5
On Becoming An Adult

After graduation, I did not know what to do as I would have to search for jobs and did not have my parents' help to do things like, helping to write a resume or to search for a job. Nevertheless, I was hired at an Insurance Company. I was not there long, as I got a Visa for the United States of America. A wish I had dreamt of for a long time. After getting the visa to the USA, I told the friends I could trust and those I wasn't sure of, I didn't. Every day, I weigh my conversation when I talked to people as telling the wrong person can sometimes go wrong. While there as a visitor, I visit my grand aunt and her family my cousins and many friends of my grand aunty, (my grandfather's sister.) The weeks were great as I was mesmerize visiting numerous supermarkets and clothing stores. Due to the weather, I had to get a winter jacket.

It was much cooler than my body wanted to feel. My aunty took me to the supermarket that had no end to them. Selling so many things I have never seen even, when I visit Canada, My first overseas vacation. At the supermarkets and clothing stores, I wanted to buy so many things but was low on cash. Aunty Norma sent money for me to buy some of the things I wanted to buy. It was weird as my aunty wanted to tell me how I should spend the money Aunty Norma sent me. I wasn't happy about that, as she spent the money for me choosing the clothes she thought I needed for me. However, due to my respect for my aunt and for older people, I kept my cool. I believe my aunt meant well, but that's how she was, and I wanted to please her. While staying with my aunt, I would visit her church and sometimes to the one I was a member of when I was back home. I met some of the most caring people, who I was so guarded of my life as I was undocumented and was not sure who I could open up to at that time. I now know I should have opened up to them as they were genuine.

After my Visa was almost up, my aunt asked me if I wanted to stay. My question to her was, can I? She said, and I quote. "I will see if a business college will accept you, and I will sponsor you if it is ok with the college to do so". I was so happy to hear those words, and I started to think positively as I was going to embark on another unknown chapter in my life. I was so happy just hearing those words. I started to feel so happy as I was going to have the opportunity to stay in America. I believe a lot of people can feel my joy when they heard words that meant hope to stay in the sawed-off Country America. A dream of a lifetime for many, and I was one of them.

In the wake of seeking out all the available right and honest resources, I came to the painful conclusion that they could not accept me as a student without a school visa and that it's really hard being undocumented in another country. If my aunt was my parent, she would be able to sponsor me. I wasn't sure how that would work, but I did not care. I just wanted to be sponsored. It was at that time my aunt asked me if I was interested in anyone at my church. I said no because my interest was in someone who was back home, and I was not going to marry anyone for a Visa. To conclude the matter, I blurt out that the latter was not an option. I also told my aunt that God would find someone for me if the guy back home was not working out. That was the end of that story, as I really wanted to find someone for the right reason.

Chapter 6
Life's Reality As An Adult

My life after being in the USA for six weeks was depressing as I was missing my family in Jamaica and longing to see my friends at church. I would try as often as I could to write letters to my parents and friends back home. I did make new church friends who were so friendly and kind. After being there for some months, I started to feel happy again and was comfortable around my new friends. I would go to their homes when invited and did not feel out of place as they were kindhearted and friendly. I told myself as long as I did not open up to any of the people I met at church, I would be ok.

After living in America for eight months, I started to feel sad again as the possibility to find work, was unsure as there was no one to confide in. (that's how I felt then). I did not want anyone to know and if there was someone that I could tell, there were few, my mouth could not say it. (I was undocumented) I was too scared to open up to anyone about not having the legal documents to live in America. I am sure someone out there wants to know what I was feeling then. However, during those times I felt afraid and was so scared to look for a job. The feeling in my mind was unexplainable during those days, and yes! in the worst way. Sweating through the process many times.

There were days when I just wanted to stay in and not go outside. At times, I would get an invitation to attend a friend's home in other States within the USA, but feeling the stress of my inner- self and in my thoughts was killing me. I just couldn't resolve anything, and it was exhausting me and was also agonizing when I would think I was going to slip up, and that would be the end of my days living in a country where many people go at no end to become landed.

I would cry a lot, feeling numb most of the time, as my brain would lie to me many times, telling me that I would never get the status to live in one of the most sawed-out Country in the world. Anyway, I prayed often and felted and believed that If I could get to fly or drive to the State of New York, I would find a job easily, and perhaps I could also see if I could find some of my Primary and high school friends who now lives in USA.

With that said, I call my mother back home just for some motherly advice. It was then my mom informed me, that a lady friend of ours knew that I was in Connecticut and was happy to house me. I was so happy, and a few months later, I moved to New York and now I would be embarking on a new way of living. The feeling was so overwhelmingly happy, and I thought then to take the greyhound, which would pass through other States that I could view while on my way to New York City where I was going. I never got to figure it out as there was so much to see and so many to choose from. I loved all that I saw.

Chapter 7

Transitioning From Home To Unfamiliar Territory

The journey was so long, and I hadn't done a trip in years when I was back home, and I was now doing one that I was unfamiliar with. The bus ride was not crammed like the buses back home. I could sit in my own seat and did not have to move over to let another individual share my seat. The greyhound was clean and had a bathroom on it. Wow, what a great opportunity to experience in such a trip? To sum up my experience, I would say I loved the journey at that time, A journey towards a better future.

When I got to the Port Union Station, our back-home friends were there to meet me, and I was happy to see them. When I got to their home it was great to use the elevator to get to the apartment. (A great feeling, I must say.) I hug her children, who were my friends, as they lived at my home, when they lived in Jamaica.

They were then young before they emigrated to the United State. They were then adults when I went to live with them. They were kind and tried their best to help me as my status at that moment was worrisome and seemed difficult. They knew my situation and that I did not want to do anything wrong that would jeopardize my opportunity to stay in America. They were amazing and deserved to know that I thank them for helping me when I needed them the most. At the time, I was young and seem uncaring. I hope they know that I miss them.

I am so sorry if I hurt them by forgetting to write back and say thanks. This was not done intentionally. I just was caught up trying to do so many things to help myself as I was trying to find a job and so much more. If my name's sake ever gets to read my book, I would like to say thanks again, and please forgive me that I forgot to write back and say thanks for all you have done for me. I am truly grateful. I never meant to hurt you.

With that said, I would like to say to my readers, and to encourage you to never forget to say thanks for any kindness extended to you. Trust me, we don't mean to do so, but it happens. We can lose friends we love and especially those we want to keep as true friends.

While in New York, I went on some interviews and got a job. On my first day to show up for work, I couldn't show up because at the end of the interview, the manager told me to bring my landed papers with me on the Monday I was to start. This was a very good job, knowing that I just entered New York, specifically "Brooklyn". When the day came, it was one of the most terrifying experiences of my life, living undocumented in

America. I recall thinking to myself, oh.... oh, if she could see my inner-self. I had an honest moment of shock waves running through my inner being, I knew there was nothing I could do. I started to pray in myself, hoping that immigration was not going to show up where I was living.

In that situation, I caved in, thinking, what did I do, I had a sick feeling then, I was in trouble, I thought, if I did show up without my landed paper, would they hand me over to the immigration officers? I felt numb within. Freezing that moment. I wanted to leave Brooklyn, New York and to disappear to another State. Nevertheless, I stayed in New York for longer. Writing about those days, is still a shivering moment for me, however, what I didn't know at the time, I was on another journey to a better life.

Chapter 8
Reflecting On Life In USA

One that now has allowed me to share my journey with you. My encouragement on this chapter of my life is, I know not all of us are born American, Canadian, English, a lot of us are immigrants from other Countries and have moved on to whichever the desired Country we would like to live in permanently and have gone on to a better life in Countries all over the globe.

To continue my ordeal of the day to the weekend had me quivering every day, even when I was out and especially on my way home, "The address that was on my application and the phone number that I placed as well." For two weeks, I was on the alert, listening for the knock on the apartment door, which I thought would be pounding, and on the other side of the door and probably hearing a voice calling for "Claudia to come out as they were from American Immigration and was here to deport me." Anyway, when the mornings came and went by, I started feeling less anxious and was able to tell myself I would not show up for work.

What I didn't understand at the time was that the manager would call to see why I did not show up for work. I could not find it in me, to pretend that everything was ok. Everything was good until the Monday morning the Human Resources manager called to inquire why I wasn't at the work. For my friends who will read my book is that, I had no papers to show at that moment. That was the day I hoped, I had those papers. I would have had a nice job for someone who just entered the Country.

I honestly did not know that the company would ask me for my papers after the interview, and I was unsure if the Human Resource Manager at that time would turn me into Immigration. If I had known then, I would not have gone on the interview. I really thought it would have been ok to apply for the job that an acquaintance of my friend told me to apply for.

Adding a little more information about that experience, let me say when the manager called and asked for me, adding who she was and why she was calling, I froze when my friend covered the phone and quietly told me who was calling for me. My friend handed the phone to me. I did not want to take the call as I felt afraid, terrified, and uneasy.

However, my limped persona took the call, as it was the right thing to do then. I shamefully took the phone and told the lady on the other end that I did not show up due to the fact that I did not have the papers she wanted to see and I would not be able to accept the job for that reason. She was sorry for my situation; however, she said she could not accept me as all companies are expected to asked for those papers. I thanked her for giving me the opportunity "for the interview" and she then wished me the best.

For days, I felt sad and was in a depressing state for a while. I thought I was going to let immigration officers snatched me up for the longest while and send me home, I was mentally alert and also made sure I, never let out that I was undocumented. I also thought that if I didn't get my thoughts together, I would make myself physically sick. What I thought and also with the help of friends, was that, I would start looking for jobs that would file for me.

Those jobs, I thought, would be a nanny or a housekeeper. Was I up for those jobs? Absolutely, as my first job back home in Jamaica was taking care of people's children at the age of ten, and was taught by my mother to clean our house well. So, I had no problem doing those jobs. Being undocumented, one has to take what every low-key job that was ok to have. It would be a job that would file for me and that was the best plan going forward. I did just that. For me at the time, this would be the job to get me starting in the right direction.

So, to those who are in the situation I have found myself in, now living in the United States of America. I would like to encourage you; by letting you know that to get the best result, you must remember that to find gold at the end of the road. Sometimes, it takes sweat and tears.

Yes, sometimes you will find yourself crying a lot because you will probably, as in my case, get a denial and have to ask for legal help. Or maybe as in others, having a smooth ride to that happy goal permanent status in one shot. My journey to permanent status was not as long as others but when any individual or family has or have to experience set-back it hurts and has in my case wondered why me?

God had brought me to an understanding at that crucial point in my life, for me to say instead, why not me? I now realize that he wanted me to know and to stay humbled that it wasn't about me but about what I could tell others about him and how he got me to write this book to help other to know that they are not alone. Nevertheless, I will also say, through my experience, I learned as well that even through the process of finding a new residency and making it through the process, one has to be very careful to try to do the best you can to live an upstanding life so, the process will favor a good standing on your behalf. However, remember to keep your life struggle to yourself until you can find someone who you can truly trust to help you sort everything out and to help you do it the right way. Through the immigration process.

Just find a good Lawyer to help you soften the stress in the process. Maybe you'll have to go back home for a time until the process is sorted out. I didn't, but some do fall into that predicament. Believe me, it will help your mental health. Yet I must say mine was easier than I thought. God was taking care of me and all I had to do, was to put my trust in him and let him control the process. And to God be the glory as I did not have to wait long as Friends that I was living with helped me to apply for a visa to stay in America and thank God and to them, I applied and got through the Amnesty program.

I was so fortunate to get one of the nicest yet stricter Immigration Officers, who did his work by grilling me so hard that I thought I wasn't going to get a temporary visa that would give me the opportunity to look for work and now be a documented resident. I strongly believe, if you believe in yourself and do what will edify the country, you want to make a home, all one has to do is to asked God and he will help you. All he asked for us to do, is to have faith and believe, if it's his will, you will get what you asked him to do for you. (Asked and it will be given to you; seek and you will find. Knock, and the door will be open unto you.) For everyone who asks receives; the one who seeks finds; and to the one who knocks, the door will be opened. (Matthew 7:7-8)

Faith and Confidence in God possess the power to move mountains

Going to Dade County in Miami to pick up my permanent resident card. (my US Green card) I got a letter from immigration that my green card was to be picked up at Miami Dade County immigration office. Getting the letter was the best feeling that day. I was so happy that I went to my boss and asked to go to Miami, Florida and she gave me the time off. Being so eager to have the card in my hand, I booked a bus ride on Greyhound from Connecticut, where I was living at the time. I didn't know where I was going but flew on a wing of hope as I was so excited. Thinking I was finally about to be a United States permanent resident. On the bus to Miami was very long but my mind was occupied with comforting thoughts. The bus stopped for all the passengers to have a bathroom break or food if desired.

I had never travelled on a bus to anywhere that long before I left Jamaica. When I went to the United States for the first time, I came through Miami and took a connecting flight to Connecticut. I noticed everyone was getting off and I was the only one on the bus. I remember the driver asking me where I was going as the next stop was where he was going to park the bus. I said, park the but! Added if there was another bus to take me to Dade County. He said no and his bus was the last. I started to panic as I was in a State that was now night and no bus to get me close to where I was heading. The driver told me that I was far away, and I mentioned that I was living in Connecticut.

The driver looked at me puzzled and, with a kind tone, told me he would go park the bus and I should stay where I was standing and he would bring his car around the front. I waited. During my wait, my mind was racing over and over with the what if's. I was talking to God in my mind, saying to God, God, I'm asking you to take care of me. I'm trusting you to help me in this unknown circumstance as I don't know what to do. I had so many obstacles that I didn't know if I could solve them. My readers, I didn't know where I was going. I was at a parking spot with a driver I knew nothing about, and I wasn't sure if I could trust him to help me, I had an appointment to pick up my Green Card the next day and was so far from where I needed to be, but most of all, I needed to get back to work.

I told the driver that I didn't know what to do about my situation at that moment, and he told me after I got into his car that he would take me to a hotel close to the immigration in Dade County.

During the drive, my mind was racing with so many more thoughts. I remember saying I thought the bus would have taken me close to the immigration building, and I was going to see if I could stay in a hotel in the area. I didn't ask the gentleman his name, and I don't remember if he told me as I was not sure what was going to happen to me. I, was in a state of confusion and just wanted to get to where he was taking me. "A hotel close by," and repeating in my mind how crazy I was not to find out everything I needed to know before getting on a bus with no idea where I was going.

The gentleman was trying hard to keep me engaged, and I was trying not to let him know I was scared. The conversation was not troubling, and after a while, I started to feel relaxed and more at ease with caution if something was supposed to happen. I encouraged myself to keep trusting God that he would take care of me. After a while, the gentleman slowly turned his face to the side of me and said, don't worry. I told him thanks and that there are not many men like him who would help a lady in dire need. My readers, I serve a big God! One who always takes care of me. I believe that regardless of my beliefs, God looked at all my faults and saw my desperate need. The gentleman could have been up to no good, but God saw it all and worked out the situation I was in.

We got out of his car and he assisted me to the Guest service Kios, this gentleman was one of a kind, it was like God allowed him to be my guardian angel from the earth. The gentleman did not leave me until I got through with the booking, and after, he asked the desk to give me a wake-up call so I would be early for the line-up.

I thanked him and proceeded to the elevator to my room. That's what God did for me. He knew I was heading into a hard rock situation and again delivered me. I thought everything would be easy after all this storm, but I was wrong.

In the morning, I got to the building and when I got in, I could not believe what I saw. The crowd was like packed sardines in a tin. There were so many people that I had the opportunity to collect my landed card, seem impossible and the crowd was behaving badly that an immigration office had to come out of the office and shout that they would not be giving out any cards or interviews and everyone should go home and return the next day. I looked around and by fifteen minutes, the place was empty and everyone was gone. Right away, I started to panic, as I knew I was in trouble. I had only that day to pick up my card and I thought quietly within me that I was going nowhere. I had to get through that day even though I couldn't figure out what to do. I had to sleep there, I thought. I would have to because I did not have enough money to linger one more day in Miami. I had a credit card, but I didn't want to use it.

I refused to move and was sitting by myself, I believe, on a seat close to the office. About five minutes I noticed a lady who seemed to be my age stopping where I was, she asked if I was going home and what I was there to do. I told her I was there to pick up my Green Card. She said she was there to pick up hers as well. She reminded me that we were asked to go home. I told her I heard what the immigration officer said, but I was going nowhere and I explained why. We went back and forth, with her constantly asking me if I was going to leave, and my decision was still no.

The immigration officer passed by about three times, telling us to leave the premises and I wasn't listening. He told us he was saying one more time and if we didn't vacate the building, he would have to call security to lead us out. I was still adamant that I was not leaving and I started to talk to God quietly in my mind. To my surprise, the immigration officer came back without the security and said to us, I'm not sure what it was about us but he was going to give us our cards. He gave it to us and we couldn't stop thanking him. He said God was with us. I knew that, and we both said yes, he's with us.

The lady thanked me for insisting that I was not going to leave and we took the Greyhound that day heading to Connecticut. We both were so happy that the lady did not realize that she got on the wrong bus and that she needed to be on a bus that was going to New Jersey. Because of the mistake, she got off the bus and we forgot to share her name and phone number. I was sad about it but she was already off the bus. I hope if she is still alive that she will read this book and remember that moment. That's what my God did for us. God wants to do the same for you and I pray that no matter what everyone is going through, my God, the God of Abraham, Isaac, and Jacob, can do it also for you, but we have to put our trust in him even when we can't see the outcome.

My encouragement to all who read this book is for you to remember this, and I am saying this from my own experiences: if it's in God's will for you to get or to receive what you ask, God is faithful to give you what you need. Believe, have Faith, and most of all, it may not come right away, but believing when you don't even see it, you will learn at that moment when you receive it that it has come when God knows you need it the most.

Moments of reflection when I was back home.

In Jamaica, I have had the opportunity to be the coordinator for a local position around my community, one in my church and many school events. I was sharp, bold, and fearless. I stood out as having the aptitude to do many things. E.g., I would do presentations in school plays, class spelling bee champion, and pray many prayers at schools and churches. Church plays were things I loved to do and I did it very well. I had and led many activities, helping out my mom when she needed to plan for events around the community. For example, Children's birthday parties, babysitting, class functions, and others. I do not remember all, and however, when children of my age were shying away from leading positions and taking on babysitting jobs and other activities, I willingly stepped into many roles at the age of nine and ten.

It was at the tender age of ten I started to know and learn what it was to know and understand my body and how it functions as a girl. Each moment, I was learning new things. I learned how to take care of my body. Especially in some of the most private ways, and that, as women and girls, men and boys grew up differently. With different body parts that look weird as we grow up to be adults. I also learned that using the bathroom outside's one's home should be done mindfully.

Women and girls should stoop over and not sit on the toilet seat. If either have to sit on the seat, seat should be padded with toilet paper or wiped with disinfection wipes if one has, or pad the seat with a bathroom paper towel. Whatever one has, use it to prevent you from going to the doctor or the hospital. I learned then, while growing up, that an adult should accompany little boys and girls when using public washrooms and to always examine my surroundings for wondering eyes.

This part of my book is so embarrassing, but I have to let my readers know that I was strangely perplexed about menstruation. My mom never talked to me about it (menstruation). So, I was not aware of the changes in women's and girls' bodies at the age when females should hear and know about the changes as we women grow older. I was also frustrated at times when it was related to menstruation, as I suffered every month with experiencing some of the worst painful moments of my life. (Maybe I was not paying attention in school), but I did now know that girls at the age of ten or even two years earlier can start their period, and usually, boys start puberty at the age of nine to fourteen.

I have to tell you, though, how I knew about someone seeing or having their periods/menstruation. It was days and months; I would see my sister putting something under her arm and steering to the bathroom. I started to watch her at the same time every month. I was alert and became very curious and wanted to know why. So, I started to watch her, taking mental notes every month. One day (as it says curiosity kills the cat) I decided to climb over the bathroom from our tenant's bathroom, which was adjacent to the one she was going in. What I saw had me like a frozen popsicle. I jumped down and yelled, mammie, (Mommy) D is bleeding! That was the day I learned the reality in a girl's/woman's body when they start to shed blood. Which is called "Menstruation."

Shortly at ten years old, it was my time to realize the inevitable. Before that, I was not aware of my body or what it would be going through. Anyway, what I remember when I started to menstruate is that I would be vomiting on and off throughout an entire day. Yes! I had it really bad. At times I felt like I was dying because I had no food in my body to bring up as I couldn't, due to me not able to keep food down. I literally was afraid to eat, because it usually would come back up. I physically had to stay in bed if my period started when I was at home.

If I were at school or out somewhere other than home, I would be vomiting on the bus. This was a very bad experience as people were staring at me as if I just rob a bank. Then, other times, I would be rushing to go to the bathroom or just in time to make it to bring-up. Yet, the worst times are when I'm in the presence of people who have nothing to do but criticize me. Sorry to focus more on living with period pain. However, it was like living with someone who was torturing me for three days, over and over again, picking my fingernail one by one as the blood spewed out. I would be crying and pressing my pillows onto my stomach for those three days. My mother usually does the best she could for me during those times. I couldn't get into a comfortable position and would just toss side by side. When I felt a little better and finally got some sleep the pain would start again.

At the age of ten "as I mentioned before" I, remember that, for me to be comfortable and at ease, I had to take Tylenol three. During one cycle, I accidentally overdosed and had to keep drinking and fighting to stay awake. Thank God, it was not my time to exist in this world. "It was an accident and only that." Amidst what I was going through, to no avail, the pain would agonizingly last at least three days straight, and I would bleed for those seven days and would go through almost two packs of lady's' sanitary napkins. The first three days was usually the worst for me.

I also remember my mom giving me some weird, tasting herbal drink to help with the pain. Mom would also have me sit on a pale that contain hot water. I would sit for an hour, on and off, to alleviate the discomfort during the painful process of the menstruation cycle. If Mom was alive, I would have told her thanks if I didn't back then, now that I have decided to write this book to tell my life's story.

Mom and I cried a lot together. I saw the tears in her eyes sometimes when I looked up for a brief second.

She was a wonderful mom who was so sorry for her child. However, she got me through those unbearable times while living back home. For those who want to hear more, let me say I saw my period for seven days in every month. Three days of which I had so much clots coming down on the first to third days. (No joke about it, heavy clots) A truly torching experience. I would lose so much blood every month that it would cause me to be anemic, and I had to take Iron supplements for years, even to this day.

Remembering, I would think it was so unfair for me to go through so much pain while others, to name a few: My mother, sister, and some of my friends, talking about them not experiencing the magnitude of what I endured. I remember as well that some of my friends would think I was exaggerating when I would talk about my experience and the dilemma I went through. (The women's menstrual-cycle world).

Anyone who has felt or is feeling the pain I felt then can understand my yearning for the day when my menstrual pain or discomfort in the cycle would end. I knew it would happen one day, and I just had to wait my turn for the menopause phase. (Just my experience) Everyone, I believe, has their own experience, and their gynecologist will explain it better in the medical world.

There were many things to learn, for example in hygiene. I had to take showers more often than I wanted to. Washing hands after being outside was something, we always had to do, along with washing our hands before eating and after coming home from school or church as well. We also had to take off our good (dressing) clothes and put on (yard clothes) which we in North America call house clothes. I'm not writing this to imply anything about any culture or any race particularly, and most of all, not to say others don't practice the above as we West Indies do, but I'm just talking about my life growing up. I hope my readers understand and read with a caring heart.

My older brothers were changing in front of my eyes, and seeing the times, they would often shave, using broken mirrors on many unsafe ledges to examine themselves. I saw hair growing on their bodies, and I saw them getting taller and muscular. As I grew older, I now can say they were filling in, as we girls would say. For men, it was ok for them to wear a beard or a mustache (Jamaicans would say). Growing older, I was understanding more about doing things that were right and wrong and the difference in choices that I would make. My mom and dad would say think, before you do or say anything.

This moment, I just remembered something and would like to share with you, my readers. I remember my mom borrowed money from a lady and my mom saw the Lady coming to collect her money from her (my mom.) Instead of telling the lady herself (what I am going to say, as at that time, I was at the kindergarten stage.)

My mother told me to tell the Lady that she was not at home and then left and went hiding. So, when the lady came through the gate, I said to the lady, (Mi maddah seh fi tell yuh dat she no deh home).

Meaning I was to tell the lady that she, my mom, was not home. I was just one of her children who was brought up to tell the truth. I did not understand at the time that I should have only said that she was not home and left it at that.

What I said embarrassed my mom. She wanted me to lie for her. Because she was surprised by the lady coming without her knowing. We didn't have a phone for the lady to call my mom or vice versa. So, I told the lady what my mother wanted me to say. Then, my mom came out of her room and told the lady that she didn't tell me to say that, I didn't hear her well. It was really awkward. I was so young at the time that I don't even remember what happened after that. Anyway, after the lady left, my mom scolded me and asked if I was stupid. Looking back, I can laugh about it now. But what I learned from that moment is that even though I was young, I should still always tell the truth if my mom realized that back then, things might have been different. So, if I were older, I probably would then have told the lady exactly what my mom asked me to do. Now that I know better. I believe I did the right thing back then.

Thinking and now remembering how naïve I was, let me open up about something I genuinely want to forget. However, now that I am older and want to bring a smile to my reader's faces, I will write. At the age of twelve or going onto thirteen, I was having a class test, and after taking the test and handing it in, my teacher called me up and gingerly letting me know and understand that "Sex" on a questionnaire box meant if I was a male or female? Instead of writing male or female, I write "No." To this day, I still cannot understand why I was lacking the basic knowledge which was obviously well-known by both genders. Even after all these years, I am still bewildered.

Nevertheless, one is never too late to learn. After that experience, I now know better and laugh every time I remember it. I was unaware, maybe I was not paying attention in school. Thus, I had to learn the hard way, as it was so embarrassing. Keep reading, and you will understand why I said No to an easy question that I should have known.

My Testimony was a cherished time for me.

At ten, I remember a lady called Sister Dobson talking to me about the man called Jesus and if he came today if I would be ready to go with him "Jesus" when he returns. (The afterlife) I told her I would not be ready. However, I knew about God through my grandmother and believed I would. However, to be sure I would give my life to Christ Jesus that day.

She continued, letting me know that Jesus came, died, and roused from the dead. She mentioned John 3V16 and asked if I believed God's words. I remember her putting her arms around my shoulder and praying for me. She asked me then to pray and asked Jesus to come into my life. I prayed, and I started crying, it was then I felt the power of God's Holy Spirit working in my heart, and just at that moment, at ten, I felt the wonderful, authentic feeling of being. It was like a shower washing with the purest of water rushing through my body from head to foot. (Only those who have experienced what I have felt that day, can testify or attest to what had and has come over me on that day).

I felt like a new person and wanted to tell everyone that I had accepted Jesus as my savior. I came to realize how wretched I was and wanted to change who I was at the tender age of ten. My sins committed were wrong against my younger brother and his actions toward me. We loved each other but at times, we were always fighting for our parents' love and other things. My youngest brother was spoiled by my mother and grandmother, and I hated to know that. My behavior after my mom went to live in Canada was unstable. I was rude to my grandmother and others and wanted to change my ways. I wanted to make things right and spend the day trying to remember if I had offended any one of my friends. I was so blunt with my words. I broke down crying, when the wrong I did, became known to me. I then promised myself and took active steps to ask everyone for forgiveness and forgive others who had offended me.

When I got home, I went to my family members who lived with me and asked them for forgiveness. Some said I did not do anything to them. Those to whom I did, forgave me. It was also only then, that I found a real sense of peace within my heart. I also realized that I was a sinner saved by God's Grace. Grace that all human race needs to find hope and forgiveness for hurting family members, friends, husbands or wives, and others we do not even know by driving drunk or driving under the influence of alcohol or drugs, and lastly, ourselves for making silly choices that are, hurtful or monstrous things classified as inhumane.

For those who do not fit into this category, you are fortunate. I would have been happy to have met you who never hurt anyone you love.

Shortly after I was baptized at my church, I experienced a hard realization that one's life can end at any moment. After accepting God in my life, I was in a walk-by shooting. The guy that got shot-laid right beside me and was hiding under a tree at the front of my house. Thank God, the shell of the bullet was what hit me under my breast, and the bullet hit the guy who was hiding under my tree. Thank God I am alive to tell of God's grace and mercy over my life.

I was fortunate and got another chance in life, to be someone who almost died at age six (slicing my right arm, causing me to receive thirty-nine stitches to close the veins and the wound on my hand) and then at the age of ten, (Missing a walk by shooting) It was then; I wondered why, God spared my life in those two instances and what was God telling me or showing me. I later got my answer and would experience why. Keep reading to find out....

During my walk with Christ, at twelve or thirteen, God's Holy Spirit allowed me to be a witness for Christ at my local church, helping with Sunday school, and being the youth secretary for our youth group and a teacher at (VBS) Vacation Bible School and had started singing at the age of nine to ten (or even earlier). All my school days, I would stand out by, singing or praying in school and in my classes. I remember my brother invited me to sing at his school and to talk about Christ to his friends, and I would visit homes in the community outside of my community, just to share God's words and to invite others to Christ. I would sing and pray on the streets in Jamaica and in the United States along with other church members, sharing with others Jesus Christ.

Hear me well, and consider this. I would never force anyone or compel anyone to follow Jesus, as the knowledge of truth and light in Jesus comes with sincerity and acceptance by Faith in Jesus and by Grace in Jesus Christ alone. This Grace from God cannot be earned but given by God and happens only, when we earnestly realize that we cannot live by ourselves and need God to guide us on our life's journey. I felt the need to share this wonderful transformation of my life with others.

There is so much to tell, so keep hanging in with me…God's love has changed my life forever, and I would not change for anyone or anything.

I lived in a ghetto (hood) environment where drugs were convenient and prevalent. Guns were accessible, killing and stealing were widespread, and life of crimes in the neighborhood was rampant. We did not see it at the time as we were so young. However, my dad saw it and never brought it to my attention until I migrated to Canada. I knew all the above was in my neighborhood, but the size of it, I now know as my dad opened up to me a long time… before he died. Telling others that my siblings and I lived a sheltered life was true. However, it was for a good reason. It was to keep us out of trouble and a life of crime. (My Dad believes one can live in the worst part of the world, but we don't have to be a product of it.)

My dad shielded us from it all by demanding that my brothers, sisters, and I stay at home and play with each other. We only had some approved friends who would come sometimes to join my brothers, who played soccer in the neighborhood. It was then, and only then, that I started to put two and two together about the crime that plagued my community. We felt as if we were like being in a box with many sides tightly sealed together. That is what our growing up was like. We were with watchful eyes that molded and shaped us. All of this played a vital part in our lives, making us who we are today. (Thanks to all who had a play in our upbringing.)

Chapter 9
And Eye Opener Experience

Entering my teenage years was eye-opening for me, and it was now a job to take care of myself. I had to think and focus on my education in high school. I went to Merl Grove High School. I met so many girls with unusual characteristics, behavior, and goals.

Few were already dating; some were focusing on their reason for being at school. Others forgot why they got the opportunity to attend a high school in Jamaica. This was a wonderful opportunity for any child growing up in Jamaica. At that time, it was children passing an exam called Common Entrance Exam that allowed them to go to high school. Now, I am told that Jamaican children no longer need to pass an exam to enter high school.

Others were just like me. Quiet and reserved in my teenage years. I grew up in a Christian world. I was bold, as mentioned at the age of ten, and was outspoken. However, I had to walk a tightrope as I had a watchful eye. A stern father figure to make sure that we did not show any bad behaviors that steered us from our upbringing. When I was sixteen going on seventeen it was a challenging year for me. I was in high school and determined to become someone destined to become an accountant or a nurse. I became none of these. I ended up working in the Hospitality industry in Canada and worked my way up to a managerial position at which I was exceptionally good at. I had goals and aspirations. To continue with the eye opener Experience, let me say,

My focus was on my studies and engaging in sports such as basketball and cricket, a game I played with my siblings. I loved Home Economics as well. Guys were interested in me at school and in the neighborhood. Some chose to engage in a conversation while sitting or standing on the bus going to places in Jamaica. For me, thank God I went to an all-girls high school. It was challenging for me to meet guys my age and others out of my league. I remember when I just turned sixteen, Mom took me aside one day, to warn me about my brother's friend who had an interest in me. Mom believed he was up to no good, and Mom was right. I heard with his mouth years later when I returned on a visit to Jamaica that he was in prison due to selling drugs, and the guy was deported from the United States of America to Jamaica. He wanted me to marry him and take him back with me. (Young girls and troubled women or anyone who is reading this book, please do your due diligence when letting boys or men into your heart).

There are genuine men in the world, but others are like snakes in a hidden forest, waiting to put their fangs into you and ruin your life. They come to cross your path, entering your life and tearing your life apart.

If you are already experiencing that path, it is still not too late to start a new journey. My encouragement is, hoping you realize that this is not the end. It is only the beginning of a new Chapter in your life that you will use to learn from and understand that some individuals do not deserve you. However, you must give your heart permission to break for your heart to heal. At the time when my mom took me aside for the talk, I was not interested in boys and was wondering why mom was talking to me about my brother's friend and not, in general, about boys. I, however, was and am so happy that my mother, for the first time, talked to me about boys as well as the birds and bees. Yet, at sixteen, I was still naive about many things.

I believed at that time, boys and girls were just each other's friends and there was nothing beyond that. Why? I took my dad seriously. An attribute of my upbringing. Let me say my life at that time was about serving God and finding my identity at the age of sixteen. My mom's birds and the bees were, that I had to be careful as some guy wants everything they can get from girls, and I should be aware of that and always remember what she was saying to me. My eyes rolled back in my head when Mom ended with, and your dad would be angry if I did the "Hokie poky."

That day, I remember feeling perplexed because I had no idea what my mom was warning me of, which was if I was talking to someone who had an interest in having sex with me. However, my mom's warning could not have come soon enough, as my brother's friend tried to kiss me. I had to pull away, and it was at that moment my mom's birds and the bees kicked in. I remember telling the boy that my dad would kill him and me if I let anyone touch me the way the boy wanted to. I want you, my readers, to know this. I was still naive as I was a church girl. He respected that and backed off.; my readers, just remember, not all guys do that. Just a note to keep your guard up. After the attempt, I wondered what I did to prompt the boy to do that. I told myself, that it must be something I did.

At the end of my thought, I realized I did nothing to bring that on. My readers, you do not have to do anything, so remember, some guys just think they should do what they like to girls or women. It was later that day, my brother told me that his friend was interested in me. What I remember about my brother's friend is that he had a girlfriend, and he wanted to leave her because he was more interested in me and wanted to stop talking to his girlfriend at the time. I remember hearing around school that his ex-girlfriend was going to beat my butt at the end of the school period. As I caused her boyfriend to leave her. I was so worried and scared that a guy in whom I did not have an interest was causing his ex-girlfriend to be so angry, and she was telling other students she was going to fight for her man. At that time, all I could think about was poor me and what was I going to do about it? All I could do was ask God to help me.

The next day, the ex-girlfriend and her ex- boyfriend caused me to be sad, anxious, and confused. I was not into things like that and did not want to be associated with those kinds of behaviors. (Fighting over a man that I did not know in that way) friends of hers and some students showed up to see the fight, but she did not. God did help me. I spent the night worrying if the girl was going to attack me when I got to school the next day. I was so scared I could pee myself. I prayed and just went to school.

While at school, the x-girlfriend came to me and told me that her boyfriend was her x-boyfriend, but she was trying to get him back. She then told me that her ex-boyfriend told her that he loves me and that if she fights me, he will kick... her butt. I told her that was news to me as I was not interested in him, so she could keep talking to him, and that I am a Christian and was not interested in any boys. A few weeks went by, and all I can remember is that I did not see him around anymore. My brother told him that I was not interested in him and about what our dad would do if my dad heard at all about it. Later in life, I heard he was doing terrible things, like doing drugs and getting a girl pregnant.

I was so happy that my mom, dad and my cousin played an intricate part in my decision to focus on my education and my life as a child of God. My advice in this chapter of my book is to let others know that you should not let any man or the threat from any woman change you. Always try hard to fight for what you believe in and take a stand for it. Please do your due diligence in finding a relationship before you let anyone in and make the wrong decisions going forward. Take your life into your hands and never let anyone take control of your life, as you grow. Take small steps if needed, and remember you can advocate for yourself. You just must try.

Women or Men can change your mind if you let them. An individual who is not strong mentally or emotionally should seek help in every way before stepping or staying into bad relationships or friends with benefits. If you do not have someone to talk to, please confide in a strong family member or a school or church council who can help you sort out your next step going forward in a relationship. Please do not make the wrong decisions. Just remember, it is your journey to finding yourself. Have faith, as you can do it if you try.

Chapter 10
Incidents That Deeply Unsettled Me

The urge to travel was getting stronger as I grew older. I had a church friend from Trinidad who was attending the University of the West Indies Jamaica. After knowing her for a while, she had a church friend who wanted to have me as his pen pal. I was communicating with him in writing and got to know him quite well, after getting to know him well. He wanted me to visit Trinidad. However, one of my church friends and my friend at the time, who introduced my pen pal to me, gave me a shocking surprise that she was getting married to my pen pal. I was devastated and confused as he wanted me to visit Trinidad.

My pen pal came to Jamaica, and we talked but never got into what caused him to marry my church friend. My heart was forgiving. I wished them the best and focused on my schooling. To be honest, I was disappointed in the whole situation and tied to a rattle in my mind: what had happened? I was also sad for a while, but thinking about it now, I came to the conclusion that God had someone better for me, and I took to heart, knowing and believing in my faith in God, for another pen pal, male friend, or a husband in the future. I realized then that I did not know what it felt like to be in love. I was disappointed but I did not cry over the situation.

I was sixteen and still young and had a long time for my future life. After what happened with my pen pal, I understood that love hurts in some cases. However, time does help with healing and sometimes brings a wealth of knowledge. Knowledge to never give your heart to someone until I was sure, that the love both feel for real. I learned, as well, that it was ok to fall out of love or infatuation when the person you think you love is not the person God has for you. Just my opinion, take your time to fall in love. Get to know each other and tell the other person who you are attracted the things that are key to growing, blossoming, and eventually healing when the relationship is passing through a moment of rocky road.

At the age of seventeen, I was still finding myself and focusing on school. I had a few friends, and they were not friendly. My brothers and sisters and my high school friend, were my friends. It was extremely hard to start a conversation. However, once I got talking, I would be comfortable in the conversation and could not stop talking if the conversation was going well. I was not a straight- A student however, I graduated from High school feeling good about myself and was ready for the life ahead of me.

My friend Citira, who I met in high school and who forever held me in her mind and heart. She was looking for me and was asking everyone whom she thought knew me and could shed some light on where I would be. She said after she left school and was getting married, she thought about me and wanted me to be a part of her wedding. However, she could not find me. I, in return, was doing the same for so long in my mind. I always had her on my mind and wondered if she got married, had children, or was even still alive. We both thought about each other as the high school days were happy with our friendship.

Sad that she couldn't find me, however, happy she kept looking for me. That is what true friendships are. My thought in this part of my life is that when you have a good friend, try to cherish that friendship, as devoted friends do not come often. One day, you will need them, or they might need you. It was after that I asked Aunty Norma if she could send a letter to invite me to Canada. Soon after that, I got an invitation to visit Canada. I went to Canada and had one of the best vacations ever. Thanks to Aunty Norma, my sister and other family members who had helped my visit to be a memorable one. With Aunty Norma I never had to worry about enjoying my stay in Albert Town, Jamaica, Canada or in the USA.

Returning home, I felt sad as I wanted to stay longer. However, I did not want to jeopardize my opportunity for a future visit, if possible. Thank God the next time I came to Canada, I landed. After returning home I continued with my schooling. Shortly after graduating from school, I started working for a short while when I visited the American Embassy for a Visitor's Visa and was able to travel to the United States of America. When I Landed in the United States, I was so happy and felt privileged to get the opportunity that many people wish for.... I saw some friends that I knew from back home and made many other new friends.

My new friends were mostly from church. I stayed in Connecticut for my vacation and visited other churches within the USA. I remember visiting Waterbury, Boston, Queens, New York, New Jersey, Philadelphia, Tennessee, Texas, and so many more while living in America.

After my two weeks were up, my aunt asked me if I wanted to stay, and I was not sure what to do as, I had just found a job and had a close friend in my life. However, it was not that I was in love with my friend at that time. I only had a strong liking for someone who was not a Christian and whose life had me in doubt and always having a worrying mind for most of the time I knew him. I would visit Jamaica often and try to get an understanding of what I thought of the relationship.

After visiting for a while, I just could not put my thoughts at rest. My friend's life, in my eyes, was questionable in so many ways, which I will not say. However, I came to the realization that one has to want to change the way one lives their life, not for me, but in my state of mind at the time, for oneself. I had also hoped he would change and give God his life. To sum it up, you cannot change someone who does not want to change going forward in getting to know and serve the God I chose and hold close to my heart.

One thing I knew was that I was not going to change for him, and he did not want to change for me either. He said I was complaining about everything. Yes, I complained about things that were wrong in my eyes and things I didn't want to be a part of. So, I listened to him telling me to find someone who was a Christian, and thank God I did.

All I can say at this point and looking back on those days, this was the best decision I have ever made. God used him to help me to be at peace with the suggested decision, and it was, and still is to me, the best choice I now know, that's what God wanted for my life to move onwards and to never look back. There are brief moments when I would wonder what has become of him and pray that God would work things out for him. I was happy with the life God mapped out for me, and I wanted the best for him as well. I was now getting older and was ready to find work. I did for a brief time, and it was at that time I decided to stay in the USA with the prompting from my aunt. My vacation was coming to an end, and I was now in another country that was new and foreign to me.

Living in Connecticut was so different. I was experiencing colder weather that I was not used to. I was away from my mom and dad and wasn't sure what I was going to do. Being away for six months, I started feeling lonely and thought about home a lot. I had no plans, as I wasn't planning to stay. I would talk to my aunty a lot and sometimes call my friend back home. I was asking my aunt how I was going to make my stay worthwhile. My aunt and I talked about my life and how it would change if I stayed and, most of all, how we would go about it to be able to execute that plan, in moving forward to become a legal Alien in America. I told my aunt marrying someone to stay was not an option.

She asked, "What about finding someone at the church I was attending to love and want to care for and see if it led to marrying that person?"

I was old school, and at that time, I had my mind on my friend at home. We still weren't sure where our life was taking us, as long-distance friendship was daunting and could go wrong. I had time to think about what my aunt suggested, which I did. However,

I believed I should continue to pray and live my life waiting to see what waiting on God's plan for my life would bring in the short or long run. How I was going to do that, I was not sure, but I was going to continue to trust God knowing that Faith is the substance of things hoped for, the evidence of things not seen. (Hebrew 11v 1)

After consoling my mind and heart with those words from God's words, I began praying and fasting. While waiting, I took a few weeks to think and work things out in my mind as well, as I also knew that Faith without work is dead. With that said, I had to do my part and continue to let God work with what I had, which was seeing me landed in the USA one day. To be honest, that was all I could envision. To me, it was enough, and I discussed my thoughts with my Aunty Miriam and Aunty Norma. Told them both of my plans to transit from Connecticut to Brooklyn, New York.

They both agreed that I could try and see what becomes of my second attempt after realizing that school, right at that time, was not feasible. I remembered that working toward seeing if I could find a babysitting job would be a step toward doing so. (Which would be to have someone to sponsor me to stay in the USA). A few months later, I made a call to my mom's friend in New York, and she was okay with housing me for a while. I was blessed to have them in my life.

Chapter 11

The Challenges I Faced And How I Handle The Challenges.

After some months had passed by, I packed my suitcase and headed to Brooklyn, New York. It was a revelation to see beautiful sights, passing state after state, as I passed along the Highway. States, with beautiful homes, farms, and stretches of green pastures spreading across as the bus cruised through the Journey heading to the beautiful state of New York City. The bus driver made stops for the bathroom and for food. The food was good at McDonald's and Kentucky Fry Chicken in one of our stops for something to eat as we scrolled through, taking in the details of the country scenery. The ride was peaceful and calming. (Junk food was tasty when I was young) However, now that I have gotten older, I don't like it as much. (About the food, I will leave it to others to make that assumption for yourselves).

I can't remember who met me at the bus station, but what I can remember was seeing the high-rise of beautifully designed buildings once I got to Port Union Square. I also remember thinking that it would really be nice to stay in this beautiful country. To encourage myself, I would think, wait on the process, Claudia, wait on it, as it will come.

Revelations that reverberated through me.

Then one day, I was in my kitchen and my land phone rang and on the other end was my brother who lives in Jamaica said there was a lady at the home I used to live, saying a friend of mine had asked her when she was in Jamaica to go to the home she thought I still lived and asked a family member of mine if I was still alive and if I was still living in Jamaica, and if I was, she should give my family member her number to call her. She mentioned, she even asked a Police friend to search for me. I was so happy I called her right away, and we talked for hours, catching up on lost time.

So, when you find your good friend, and I say a good friend, and if they find you, knowing they thought you were lost. Also, they have moved their teeth and nails so they can get in touch with you. Do not worry, as my take on this is that good friends are hard to find. My friend Citira, never stopped looking for me until she found me. Good friends will never stop until they find you. Just never stop looking. It will be the best experience knowing that person cares.

Deeply disorienting moments in my life.

It was after a car accident, that I was able to trust someone in the most intricate private part of my life. After the accident, I had to allow myself to trust someone. I told no one, that includes my family, church friends, and most of all, not my strict parents. My dad taught me not to trust men (but I can say not all men rape women), just predators and selfish ones who just want what they can get and, in my case, take my innocence away.

This had destroyed my life, in so many…many ways, causing me to make some of the biggest mistakes, especially in the way I looked at men. (I mean, I see them as selfish and self-centered.) As I grew up, I talked to the wrong ones, which should have been a red flag to me when I saw the things they wanted and the way they treated me.

The ones I disliked were the good ones, but my not feeling love for them got in the way and clouded my mind. All of this was before I grew up to be the lady I am today. I have made some mistakes in life, and not having my sister to talk to about many growing-up issues made me toughen up and grow up. Amidst the mistakes I made, I learned from them. Some brought tears, and some showed me how God took care of me, molding and reshaping me into a beautiful Christian life. One I would now never sell for anything or anyone.

I grew up with a decent upbringing and had to be aware of my surroundings because of what had happened to me when I was very young and to also think about what was right and wrong before I did anything. Especially when it has anything to do with the male gender. I, however, at that stage in my life, was naïve. This caused me great struggles to open myself to people. I was close to both men and women. However, as a teenager, I would wonder about many things and would never dare to confide in my peers about the many things I was going through at that tender age. My sister left and was living in Canada.

The decision to trust someone to talk about the rape with the first person took an accident. Then later, it took courage to talk about the rape to a second person... my Psychotherapist. It was hard, and I was breaking down in my mind ...like opening a gate that was closed for years and tossing the key to the bottom of the ocean. Uprooting years of pain that I buried at the bottom of the deep ocean within me that day was not easy. I remember crying when I got home and experiencing relief after I let it all go.

Remembering how I struggled for years and built the nerve to talk about it was heartbreaking and gut-wrenching. I tried many times to tell someone, anyone, but could not get the courage to do so, which caused me to bury it even deeper. However, after the accident in 2015 and as I got older and stronger physically, mentally, and emotionally, I started to feel empowered and strong to open up about the rape to an insurance Psychiatrist. It was the first time I felt such peace and was ready to open up about my anguish.

After telling the psychiatrist, I felt I could muscle the courage to tell my family and others and pray they would not judge me or be disappointed in me. It was extremely hard. I just couldn't talk about the rape until after many years of counseling.

My psychotherapist got me to open up even more, and it was then I got the courage to tell my son, my husband, and others. I know I have to tell my family before my book comes out. I pray that God will give me the courage to open up to them. I am still waiting for the moment to tell them. I hardly slept that night after I told my Psychotherapist, re-living the moment-by-moment of it all. Thank God the morning came because it seemed like a long night. I was just thinking about what I would say if I told them the details of my situation. It was now another day. What that meant for me is I now feel no fear of living to see another day.

I blamed myself for years, wondering what I did wrong. until my psychotherapist nurtured me back from the worst experience a young girl could have gone through. I hated this person for the longest while for making my life miserable. I thought back then and was thinking now, and I had to forgive him because I am a child of God, and I have to forgive others, even when they are the worst of scum in life. Forgiveness is real, I can say, as forgiveness brings peace and healing. Deep down, I had despised him and kept the hate inside for years, and My Psychotherapist taught me how to stop blaming myself and to use my horrific experience to challenge myself to champion the hurt and turn it into strength to help others who had gone through a similar ordeal and is facing the reality of that moment.

I had some bad friends and had to peel off many layers as I got wiser. Sixteen was supposed to be the best time of a teenager's life. Instead, I felt scared as a girl growing up. I also had the feeling that I was damaged goods and made stupid mistakes. Looking back, I realize I had let my guard down for some vulture to steal from me and destroy me mentally, physically, and spiritually.

Chapter 12

Emotionally Seismic Moments Good/Bad

Throughout the process, I was misjudged many times, and a lot of terrible things were said about me that I wanted to forget. But for me to forget, I had to forgive myself and forgive the culprit.

That was not me, and I had to stay calm. I couldn't blast back, even though I wanted to. I may have lived a sheltered life, and I let people into my life that I never should have let in. However, God chose my life's journey, which was pre-destined by God before I was born, and now that I was here in the flesh, God had allowed me to go through each and every one of the choices as I grew older year after year. The troubles and trials were mine to sort out and never to pass and stop there again. I would have to sum it up as it was mine to bear. What happened was I let people who I should not have let become my friends. After all that, I still meet people who just want to continue to destroy my life in God and my reputation as well.

You see, God was taking me through a journey that was showing me how to choose friends, both men and women, wisely. I have learned to discern and trust men who have integrity while calling out those who have none. It was hard and worrisome, but thank God that I had the patience to learn. I have come across men who filled that shoe and others who did not. Any of the above criteria could be my friend, but to give my heart to someone, to the point of marriage, and to be my Husband, friend, and partner, he had to be special.

I did meet many male friends to give my heart to over the years. The ones I cared about were not Christians and, in my opinion, did not love God the way I did. I didn't want to have the one that I eventually chose to have as a husband, divorcing me when things went wrong. I wanted someone who he and I could work it out. I had met a few guys over the years before I met my husband, and looking back, and I now realize that all the others were not God's will for me. All I could do was to accept my life then and continue praying for Mister Right. Mr. Right had to be from God and love God as I do. God answered me a year after I left marrying someone totally in his hands.

Perry, my precious gift from God.

Let me open up to my reader about the year I met my handsome, caring husband, who I, at the time, did not know would be the man I would marry. I met my husband in the fall of 1998. I was at church, sitting in a theater-like church building on a Sunday morning. That day, I was sick and coughing so much that he turned around a few times, asking me if I was okay. I politely turned to face him and said yes, I was ok. I wasn't lying; I just wanted him not to have pity for me. He, however, kept asking me if I was sure that I was ok because I did not sound like I was feeling ok.

In my mind, I was thinking, why was this guy asking me so many times if I was ok.

Anyway, I forgot about that Sunday morning and went to work the Monday morning, not thinking about the moment of concern bestowed by this nice gentleman who sat beside me, disturbing my morning worship. The next week, I went to church, and the seat I usually sat in had the same guy in the row I sat. I just thought it was just a coincidence that he was sitting close to me again. I said hi, and he said hi, and we enjoyed church that day. At the time, I was in a church group that held concerts often at the church and would host concerts in Canada and in the USA.

I don't remember seeing him attending any of our group concerts. Nonetheless, every Sunday, he was in the seat next to me or two rows down. Then, one day after church, we started a conversation, and he was telling me that he had Sisters who were married to West Indian men. I wasn't thinking anything about it at the time. Then, one day, he told me he had a session with the Pastor because he wanted to become a member of the church I was attending. I thought to myself that I didn't remember seeing him at church, and I didn't remember him wanting to become a member of the church. Anyway, he told me he was supposed to attend another church, but he could not find it. He noticed our church and decided to attend. (My readers see how God works?)

Then the big day came. The day I asked him if he wanted to come to my house, as he had a meeting with the pastor again. I gladly asked him if he wanted to come home with me, as his meeting was later in the evening, and he was living an hour away with his dad at the time. I thought, Oh no! I did not ask my sister if it was ok to invite Perry, the young Greek man I met at church.

I remember letting him know that I had to ask my sister, if it was ok to invite him to our home. I remember my oldest sister's words (Claudia! You don't even know if the guy eats West Indian Food). My lightbulb in my head went on. You're right, and I forgot to ask, I said. She, my sister, said; next time, you should ask before you invite someone to our home.

I felt awkward at the time and wondered how I was going to ask Perry, but then my sister said to tell Perry it would be ok. I was so relieved I quickly picked up my feet in my hand and hurried back to him a few minutes later to let Perry know that it would be fine to come home with us before his session with our Pastor. At the time, I was so happy to be of service to someone who needed my help. Perry did not have a car, so we all traveled together in my sister's car. When we got to our apartment, I welcomed Perry to our home, and we all had dinner.

After dinner, Perry sat on the sofa beside me. He told me that he had been praying for a wife for four years, and when he saw me, God told him that I would be his wife. I wanted to be polite, so I listened and smiled.

However, I thought, why didn't God tell me as well? Perry, at the time, was at peace with what he said, as his next words were, Claudia, all I ask is for you to pray about it. I told him I would. After that day, he would call me every day. We exchanged phone numbers and started the phone dating process. We spoke on the phone for hours at the time and sometimes didn't want to get off the phone because we were compatible together.

We loved talking on the phone so much that, at times, I had heavy eyes for work the next day. However, staying up late did not interfere with my ability to function at work. I was not sure how it went for Perry and forgot to ask him as we didn't care. We would go for tea often, and sometimes, we would just sit for hours and enjoy talking to each other and being together. Perry was a romantic, and I love his heart. He was so special, and I believe that there was no one like him to me.

Let me say, and of all the male friends I ever dated, Perry was exceptionally good for the husband type. He and I felt that he was my night and shining armor who came to rescue me. I felt like a princess when I was around Perry. He dated me with total respect.

Never touching me inappropriately. He (I would tell myself) was such a gentleman, and he's still the same even to this day. In my eyes, he was really a child of God. You see, long before I met Perry, I had asked God for a Christian husband, as I had dated someone who was not a Christian. I was praying for signs and for God to show me some type of indication of the possibility of a husband in him.

Even after a year, God did not give me any indication of marrying any guy that I knew. I did not feel right about the other guy I was talking to; in my mind, something was off, and I couldn't wrap my brain to figure it out. It's a true saying. (love/infatuation is blind) But thank God, he worked it out for me by using that guy to tell me to marry a Christian guy. That was when I truly believed that that guy wasn't the one for me.

I remember asking God for a sigh, and God used that guy's words to convince me that he, wasn't who I needed. I was so crushed at the time. Now, I see it was for the best.

Anyway, I knew God had someone better for me, and most of all, he would be a Christian. I was comfortable with that promise as God's word said, "For I know the plans I have for you declares the LORD, "plan to prosper you and not to harm you, plans to give you hope and a future. (Jeremiah 29:1) every time I remember those words I feel blessed and grateful to God that he has listened to my prayers. I will say to all who read my book that God does answer prayers. What we all need to do is to trust and wait patiently for God to give us the ok. I know for sure Perry is God's blessing to both him and me. We were made for each other.

We got married a year or a year and a half after we met. I remember the evening when Perry asked me to marry him. My sister and a church friend of ours who lived on the same building were by us at the time. Perry knocked on the door, and I remember my sister saying that he was there. He mentioned that he brought something for me. Perry knew I loved chocolate, and he brought me some almost every time we saw each other.

But before that day, my sister was in our kitchen when we heard a knock at the door. Looking through the apartment peephole, seeking a man holding a bouquet of one/two dozen red roses, my sister opened the door and took the roses, which had my name on them. I heard my sister calling me as I was in my room. When I opened the door to my room, my sister met me with the red roses. I was like, for me? She then handed me the vase, and I smiled. I remember her jokingly saying, "If you don't want him, I will take him." (My sister is married to a wonderful man as well.)

I smiled and took the roses to my room.

Chapter 13

More Surprises From A Man Who Loves Unconditionally

Another day, I was at work when the Human Resources Department called me to the office. When I went to the office, one of the managers handed me a vase of white roses. I don't remember which one told me the guy who sent me the roses is a keeper. I smiled just as I had the day with my sister. I called and thanked Perry. I took the vase to the office and carried on with my job. After I got home, my sister said that that guy loves you, and I agreed. After the bouquets from Perry, we went on so many different dinner dates and more. To be honest, I have loved every hour, day, and month that we have spent together. Perry loved doing Picknicks, and we went to many of them when we were dating. Perry and I, along with my sister, her husband Kenneth, family, and friends, planned a beautiful wedding day and now hold beautiful pictures to relive it day after day. (Thank you! Kenneth and Yvonne and all who helped with that day.)

After we came back from a beautiful honeymoon in Montreal, we went to the apartment Perry was renting in Toronto. He made it so nice; I couldn't be prouder of him. He was at the time and still is a very handsome handy guy. I got to see how loving, how handy, and what a beautiful person he is as we blossom in our life together as a married couple. I will never say married couples don't have their disagreement at times, which we do. However, it is how we handle disagreements and how we agree to raise our children, collectively in our marriage. Most of our feelings towards each other are about why we need to change or curve our characters and the way we live to make our marriage and relationship last to the golden years, which some of us know can be done.

For Perry and I, we depend on our relationship to work by keeping God at the forefront of our lives on a day-to-day basis. We believe and remain steadfast that we cannot do anything without God's help. (John 15:5) Many will disagree. However, that's just how I run with my life. Nevertheless, I agree with disagreeing as all have different personalities and upbringings that play some kind of role in how we handle situations.

Before dating Perry, I was in a long-distance relationship with a guy in Jamaica, and I would be so unhappy every time I got a clue that he was being unfaithful to me. I refuse to mention his name. I have to be truthful that the more I prayed for that relationship to work, the more God would allow things to happen that gave me bad feelings all the time. I couldn't sort things in my mind as I had gut feelings that something was wrong when I was living in the USA and even after I moved to Canada.

God had to use that individual to take me away from that person. Do I regret that the relationship went sorrowful? Absolutely not. On the contrary, it was the best thing that ever happened to me. I can breathe a breath of fresh air, writing this part of my book. Let me say thanks to you, God! Knowing what I know now about that person, I am now saying I don't believe I should waste any more lines of my book to talk about any other man than the sweet and wonderful man I met a year after I left Jamaica, which is my husband.

Dating Perry was and is a beautiful story, and for me, it is worth telling. He took care of me from day one when I met him. He showed me what a relationship and love feel like. I strongly believe that if I was married to the other guy or any other, I would have been divorced already. We all have moments in our lives that sometimes cause friction in our relationships, but it's what and how we deal with what we are going through. I felt and still feel secure in our relationship even today as I've found someone who will stay and take care of their other significant other, in sickness and in health, till death do we part. One has to be thankful for finding someone who has your best interest at heart. I am thankful for having Perry in my life.

Yes, I am married to a wonderful man, and I strongly believe that he is from God. My God is good and has been a strong tower in the days when we need him. When we have disagreements, it should help us to understand and grow from those disagreements.

That's what I had with Perry. You see, God knows who is his, and when the road gets rocky, he has and is still there for both of us. That's the comfort I find in having God as my guide in my life, my marriage, and my journey in life, especially in our trying moments. Everyone in life has a choice of who's for them, so my readers, it's just my life, and I am just sharing my journey with you and how I live my life with God. I fear him and hold his precepts in my walk as I continue each and every day.

I have not and will never tell anyone how to choose their partner. However, I can say to you who choose to read this book that it is wise to always be on guard, as not every male or female who comes into your life is genuine. They are absolutely a part of your journey. Nevertheless, please take the time to know such a one before giving your heart. Our hearts are delicate. Even though it is ok to have your heart broken, it should be for the right reason. My heart had been broken three times.

Anyway, to learn (in my opinion), I go through things and the hurt from my past and take out of it all what I need to learn from those experiences. However, I thought and would like to say to you, my readers, that it is your journey to learn and embrace the good and bad of your life experience and to expunge those that should never be repeated.

I hope no one ever repeats their mistakes, as it gets harder the second time around. Nevertheless, just know that mistakes are our learning tools.

Therefore, your mistakes do not and should not define you. I know it is difficult, but never cease to keep working at loving yourself first. It will help you go forward. Know and remember these words, and you will eventually get them right if you keep trying. I believe that with God, all things are possible. Just ask, believe, and trust that he will keep you, more even when you trust him in all you do.

After marrying Perry, we wanted to have a child. My work schedule was overwhelming, and my body was tired, and I just could not get pregnant due to my long and difficult schedule. So, we decided to try out intrauterine insemination. Ok, we will try. We came to an agreement and sought help from our gynecologist. He gave us a referral to see a reproductive endocrinologist, and we had the appointment. We did get to talk to the doctor, and we set up a date to start the process.

Two weeks later, I noticed that my period was late. I thought to myself, "Your body is so weird, Claudia" and brushed it off. The next day, I was at the pharmacy and decided to buy a pregnancy test, and I was not going to let my husband know, just in case my body was just playing games with me.

I remember waiting until my husband was sleeping, tip-toed to the bathroom, pulled out the kit, and waited for the result. I wasn't hopeful due to the many kits I have been disappointed in. Anyway, I had my eyes closed because I did not want to feel sad again because I did not see positive results. I then told myself to open my eyes, and reluctantly, I did, and I could not believe what I was seeing. My eyes could not stop looking. I asked if this was for real or if I was seeing doubles. I slowly breathe in and out to calm myself down. I then opened the door and shook my husband, waking him up and telling him that I was pregnant. I remember he looked bewildered, and it took him a while to grasp what I was telling him. Yes, I was finally having a baby. I had to cancel the procedure. Thank God for answering our prayers.

I had my handsome son in two thousand and three in the year of SARS. After being discharged from the hospital, I got a call from the hospital to return because they wanted to make sure my son did not contract the virus. I had to be adamant that I was not going to take him back as I tried so hard to have him, and because he was born in that year, I should put his life in jeopardy? "No way, I told the nurse at the end." She then agreed that as long as he wasn't showing any signs, it was good news. I stayed in for six months so I would not expose my son to whatever was out of my four walls. I kept up with his doctor's appointments, and that was satisfactory for me.

At six months, I took my son to the doctor because he was running a high fever, and no matter what I did, the fever was not tempering. When I got to the doctor's office, he took my son right away and told me to take him to Sick Kids Hospital. I took a taxi, and they admitted him as his fever was so high. They thought he had meningitis. For two days, I was weak from crying because the doctor was just poking needles in my son, trying to figure out why my child's fever would not subside. After two days, their findings were that he picked up a virus, and they did what they had to do, and I was able to take him home. Thank God!

When my son was five years old, I got a call to meet my husband at Sick Kids again. I called my husband, and he told me that our son could not walk. I quickly left work and went to the hospital. When I got there, my husband said they were running tests on him, and he wasn't sure what was going on with my son. I had to stay strong again. Asking God for strength and grace to see this moment in my life. My son was admitted for a week because they could not discharge him because the hospital could not figure out, once again, what was happening to my son. My husband and I had to sleep at the hospital for a week with no shower. I had to buy clothes at the shop there.

Sick Kids ran test after test to find out why he could not walk. My son spent his birthday in the hospital.

Sick Kids was great, and they gave him a present on his birthday. That was a great encouragement for my son and helped us, my husband and I, to feel someone at ease. My boss at the time sends my son a gift for his birthday as well.

After some days and the many poking of needles, we were told that he had influenza A. Throughout that phase of our life as parents, we still had to trust God for his grace so that we could still have our son. My son was discharged, and we were thankful for the opportunity to take him home once again. The enemy was testing us, but God was giving us the strength to go through the test of our life and faith. Because my son was getting sick a lot and I was always panicking a lot, my husband was the calmer one and would try to calm me down many times. I just did not want to lose my son.

Time passed, and everything with my son was going well. He was smart as a toddler and as a teenager, and I was so proud of him then, the enemy started to attack his mental state. He graduated with honors in middle school and went on to high school, doing well as expected. Then, we were tested once again. His mental state (OCD) was beyond our capability. Many times, I had to fall on my knees to consult God again for things I could not understand. This was way beyond my capability to handle. I was lost and did not know how to solve the situation that was new to me as a parent. My son was banging his head on the walls and folded, curling up in the corner of his room. Screaming that he was going mad. It was painful to see my son walking down the stairs, holding his head, screaming that he could not take what was going on in his head.

He doesn't want me to say anymore, to sum it up. His mental state was challenged, and he's still working on himself, regardless of how it set him back, as it is hard for him to decide to search to find what he would like to do with his life due to his mental health. My husband and I will wait patiently as we can only leave all our situation in God's hands and let him work out my son's future the way he sees fit. On this issue, I will say mental health is real, especially with the youth of today, and as parents, all we can do is support our children the best way we can and leave the outcome to God. I know some will not agree with me, but I will speak on this matter because I am one of the affected moms. I sympathize with every parent who, like me, doesn't know what to do.

Chapter 14
Profoundly Jarring Experiences

In the United States, I have accepted positions such as Sunday School Teacher and Assistant Youth Leader. Here in Canada, I was the Director of Multicultural Ethnicity along with My Husband at the Church of God of Prophecy in the West End of Toronto. I was also part of a Gospel Singing Group that sang in Canada and the United States. I sang in my country as well, and I got the opportunity to do so everywhere I went. I love to talk about God everywhere I go and at every opportunity I get to do so.

After arriving in the United States, I started to hang around friends who were not a part of God's kingdom and purposes. I went to functions and home parties that had drinking and smoking, it wasn't so much the drinking and smoking that made me uncomfortable — it was the way people were fondling each other while dancing that really unsettled me. Knowing the people dancing this way was with some random person who came to the party and was not their boyfriend or spouse. When one feels uncomfortable, that should be our cue to leave. I never drank or smoked, it was just being around an unfamiliar environment with such loose behavior that had me feeling foreign and gave me a weird feeling.

People would think they know me. Some were asking me to attend parties and functions many times, trying to change me to convince me that I need to try the world. Some, I would attend but because I was now the girl who was able to feel out of an environment or situation, I would politely excuse myself and leave. I was at times called boring or holier than thou.

However, few of my friends in my teenage years hated me because of who I was. I love and still love those who stayed my friends, even today. All it was that I could not share their lifestyle. The ones who understood me and respected my views were and remain my true friends.

Some of my peers' lifestyles during high school had me so uneasy many times. Choosing friends over my Christian beliefs was not an option. To elaborate, some situations and behaviors were troubling my mind and I knew I just could not please others, I had to act on my instincts at times, such as refusing and leaving dance that's called a party. This would cause me to lose my friends or those who are so-called friends. I was never, nor better than any of my friends. I know that when I examined myself in my mind, all it was that I was different and had a different lifestyle.

I felt at the time, that I could not lead any of these friends of mine or people that I had just met to Christ because I was not being a follower of Jesus but a follower of my flesh and what other people wanted me to take part of, when I was around them. I had to ask God to forgive me for my actions and thoughts. I shook my head many times during my young adult years, which was very scary. Deep down inside, I knew I still had to display the same behaviors and life walks, showing a Christ like behavior every day, even to this day.

My grandparents, my parents, family members, and heartfelt friends helped to shape and mold me. I had to be aware then and now of how to conduct myself before others and before God. Before, I would try to enjoy the things of this world more than being myself, knowing I was brought up differently. Nothing was wrong with going to parties and gathering with friends, however, when I was with others, I would sometimes end up on the wrong path, doing what I was not brought up to do. I use to go to dinners with friends, but sometimes, their conversations would leave me questioning myself or feeling uncomfortable—especially at gatherings where there was too much alcohol or illegal activity. Therefore, I had to many times, make the decisions to pull myself away from whatever would distract me and my belief and life in God.

All who know me know that I am a child of God, and God has to come first in my decisions for all situations in my life. We who serve God cannot indulge in the things of this world, e.g. (Doing everything and anything for the love of having money or pleasure.) making or having money is ok. However, it should not make us feel superior above others, especially when we obtain it illegally. Having wealth can sometimes create a sense of distance or superiority, but it should never take us to that level to not care about others. I say that to say this as, I have been with others who have placed money over their friends and I know the feelings so very well and it does hurt when you have known those friends since you were young.

Chapter 15

Delve Into The Sentiments That Shaped Me In This Phase In My Life's Journey

One should weigh the pros and cons of a relationship and if the con is more an indication that would cause trouble or uncertainty in friendship, it would be up to us to choose to do what is right. We cannot keep falling from God's grace and his protection over our lives. There are times I had to rededicate my life to God and therefore had to once again, focus on his purpose for me as a Child of his. My loyal friends and acquaintances know me well and always encourage me to follow God and never to deviate from his words.

My life was and still is governed daily by reading God's word and following his book according to his promises and discipline. As I read, I continue to ask for God's mercy over my life and that of my family. Serving God is one of the most graceful experiences in my life. I enjoy the peace he gives me as I encounter daily challenges. Serving others gives me great pleasure the older I get. What I have learned is that when you serve others who have been there for you, that's not really serving according to his words, for what benefit it is, when you give to others when they don't need the help and forget those who truly need your help. I know sometimes we need to show people who have our best at heart that we are thankful for what they have done for us. For those who have helped me to this day, I say thank you.

However, he recognized the help to those who truly need your help when they have no mean to help themselves.

As Matthew 25:35-45 say, 'For I was a hungered, and ye gave me meat: I was thirsty, and ye gave drink: I was a stranger, and ye took me in: naked, and ye clothed me: I was in prison, and ye came unto me.

Then shall the righteous answer him, saying, Lord, when saw we thee a hungered, and fed thee? or thirsty, and gave thee drink? When saw we thee a stranger, and took thee in? or naked, and clothed thee? Or when saw we thee sick, or in prison, and came unto thee? And the king shall answer and say unto them, Verily I say unto you, in as much as ye done it unto one of the least of these my brethren, ye have done it unto me. My thoughts on all this are that, you should do your best, to do what is right in the sight of God, which means for me, is that, we should always try to help those who cannot help themselves in any way we can and do it from the heart and God will bless you for helping the needy.

Moments of concern/ Living in New York City

Let me open up about the prick of my conscience when I find my time is not occupied in the best way in God's eyes. At times, I would be watching TV or a movie with lots of clippings with disturbing action and profanity and I feel compelled to stop watching as what I was watching is not of God, but of the world. I would stop because of the conviction that God placed in my mind and heart. I know that some people will not agree with how I determine what I am writing and my reaction to this in this sentence, but those who can attest with me understand. They want me to do what is best for my life as I have to account to God of all my actions in life.

Giving God the most of my days makes me feel the most satisfied. I crave daily to be what he would like me to be as I go through this world we live in. Life is not the same in this era of the twentieth century.

Nevertheless, we should always follow our hearts and minds when dealing with or encountering situations that require us to take a second look in our daily walk or journey. Now, let me continue to talk about my life since I decided to go to New York City. New York was scary where I stayed, but I had God watching over me when I traveled anywhere in Brooklyn. The Grace of God kept me, and I am thankful to him for keeping me through the bustle of it all.

I stayed in New York for a while and found a job in New Jersey. I worked with a family that hired me to take care of their two children and wanted to sponsor me as I was undocumented.

It was great working for the family, but due to unforeseen circumstances, I had to leave and, therefore, look for another job. I eventually found a job in another State, which I would like to forget. After I was hired to babysit their children, I thought at the time that it was going to be great working for this family. However, an encounter at a cottage vacation had me scared of this family.

As I was ready to go to bed, the father of the children made me feel scared as he made a pass at me. I didn't sleep well; I was just worried about closing my eyes. I was so fearful as he wanted to sleep with me. His wife was just a few stairs up about the basement when he made that pass as me. I want to open up to my readers as I know some of you have experienced what I have gone through in this job. However, never think that you have to give in because you need the job. Just remember that you can leave and find another job.

Don't give in, as down the road, you will regret it. Stay strong and be yourself.

After telling my church friend, who is also a friend of my sister's, she helped me get a job close to her in Long Island. She was the friend I which I could have for life. However, after leaving the United States, we did not communicate, as I moved to Canada after living in Connecticut for a long time. However, we saw each other, in a year when she came to Canada. It was good to see her again. Let me talk about my time living in New York specifically, "Brooklyn". At the moment, I don't remember how long I lived in Brooklyn. I believe I lived with my mom's friend while working in New Jersey. My church friend and I would go to church as often as we could. Going to church in Brooklyn, New York, was such a great experience and such a blessing. I remember being asked to sing a few times at the Church I attended and to God be the Glory as singing at times was a humbling experience. Every time I sang, I would be so blessed and would feel revived to keep me through the next day and sometimes even through the week.

I would visit my friend sometimes after church as I was not living far from her. I remember spending a night at her home with her roommate. Her roommate had a mental issue. I didn't know at the time that her roommate had a mental health problem and that night while staying with my friend and sleeping in the living room the lady had a breakdown. That night, I heard my friend say stop to her roommate. I jumped-up and asked with a puzzled reaction, wondering what was going on as I was still in a sleep state. My friend yells for me again to go get help. On that specific night, her roommate started to attack her. I saw it for myself and was then hearing my friend who was pleading to her roommate to stop hitting her. She was still yelling for me to help her.

I didn't know what to do, however, all I could do at that moment was to dash out of the house and knocked on a neighbor's house to call 911 for me, I was explaining to the Lady who came to the door, what had happened and to asked the lady, to tell 911 to hurry-up, as I wasn't sure what the roommate was doing to my friend. The lady that came to the door told me that the police were on the way. I did not go back to the house as I was still anxious and scared.

When the Police and the Ambulance came, they took the roommate and she was taken to the hospital. I was told she was off her meds; she was in the hospital until she got better to go home. I don't remember if I spent a night over after that day. My take on that day and moment is to let my readers know, who is also a sufferer with mental issues, that we should stay on our meds until we are told to get off them.

I have taken the right approach that if anyone desires to be off meds or getting your doctors to agree with you to get off your meds. It's ok. I personally know now what being off prescribed meds can do to anyone who should be on them. I will say that it's an unpleasant feeling and can lead you to do things you would not normally do if you were on them. To this day, I still remember that incident and will not want to experience it again. However, my friend and I would meet at church and would communicate by phoning each other.

My friend and the church members that I had were true friends and were rare. We would gather together at church functions and had the best times visiting each other's homes or at a fast-food location. I had other friends in Connecticut who were rare and true friends as well. I worshiped and sang at both churches. I sang more in Connecticut. I was ready to stay in Brooklyn at the time, but the experience with many circumstances in my path changed my decision. Also, when I was in New York, I missed my family in Canada and Jamaica, as well as the friends I met in Connecticut.

Aunty Norma was now living in Connecticut at that time, and I couldn't wait to see her, as she was moving to the United States when I was in New York City. The job my friend helped me to find was a good job, but I wasn't sure what was going to happen as my job at the time was getting in my way when it came to attending church on the weekends. The other jobs I had before gave me the option to be home on the weekend.

It was during that time and moment that the family I was living with helped me come to the understanding that I could apply for amnesty in Florida. I spoke to Aunty Norma, and we decided it would be the opportunity I was looking for. I came to Florida when I first visited the United States. There are a lot of things I don't remember as it has been so long since I left the USA. This is due to loving Connecticut more than New York or anywhere else in the USA. I remember more of my life in Hartford, Connecticut. After leaving a bitter-sweet departure, I realized that I had hurt the family that I stayed with. I wasn't sure what I did wrong at the time of my departure when I left New York City. I wanted to get back to Connecticut as my aunt and most of all the people in Connecticut I was told, were asking when I was returning.

Chapter 16

Deciding To Start The Process To Leave America For Canada

Some thought I was ready to leave New York because I now have my United States Temporary Landed status or have some form of stability.

However, the real reason I was leaving for Connecticut was that I missed my family and was feeling depressed in Brooklyn, New York. Brooklyn, NY, was not much different from Hartford, Connecticut, when it came to a desire to find a comfortable home and life. The difference was that my aunt had a house, and I lived in an apartment. I was grateful for the opportunity to experience living in another State. Unfortunately, I had to take the stairs most of the time as the elevator for the Apartment broke down so often in Brooklyn. I was so tired of using it, as the stairwell was so unpredictable. Guys would be sitting on the stairs smoking hard stuff and had me scared of the what-ifs. This was mind-boggling and I had sleepless nights that I chose not to share with anyone. I just pray that I haven't offended anyone who had helped me get to where I am now.

What added to the decision to leave New York was me experiencing a day when there was a fire on the building I lived, it made me so scared that I could not sleep well that night and onwards. I was just so scared after that and had never overcome the encounter until the day I left New York to live in Connecticut and then to Canada, a day I never regretted after making the transition. After living in Connecticut for a while, I decided to ask my sister to file for me.

Chapter 17
Another Opportunity Of A Life Time

My sister said she was filing for my parents, which would allow her to file for the unmarried children as well. I thank God for such an opportunity and for allowing me to eventually have a permanent country to call my home. At that time, as I was writing my book, I remember starting to feel relaxed and at peace, believing that I would finally be reunited with my mom, dad, and siblings once I received my landed papers for Canada. Back then, that's all I could think about. I thought often through the process how happy I was going to be and that I couldn't wait to leave the United States of America. I loved living in America, as America gave me a start in life, and have met wonderful people that I still love. Nonetheless I wanted to be around my family who live in Canada.

My thoughts on the process and journey are that you should never stop praying and hoping to become a Citizen of any country that will give you the opportunity to live and work in their Country. It can happen. However, remember it's not your birth country so live your life while you are waiting with honesty, decently and wisely. Pray for God's will to take over and work things out for you. Psalm 27:14

"Wait for the Lord; be strong and take heart and wait for the Lord." Wait only upon God as all our expectations and help comes only from him. Isaiah 40:31. But they that wait upon the Lord shall renew their strength; they shall mount up with wings as eagles; they shall run, and not be weary; and they shall walk, and not faint. My readers, take courage in these words.

Chapter 18

A Reflective Period Marked By Both Joy & Sorrow

While waiting for the process of migrating to Canada, I continued to focus on saving to help with the transition when that day arrived. It was essential not to spend, as I was also waiting on the final process, which was already in the works. "Getting myself landed in the United States." Let me recap more about...

Having my first interview in Miami for a chance to a better life.

Let me continue talking a little more about what I remember going to my first interview in Miami Dada County. I book a flight with my mom's friend's daughter. I can't recall all the details of that day; however, what I remember is that I was sitting waiting to see an immigration officer. It was scary as I wasn't sure if the interview would land me back home. The reality facing me was that I was an illegal alien seeking to get a chance to live in the United States permanently. I was very nervous and praying for God to take pity on me and bless me with a caring Immigration officer.

What I can recall on that day was that I was shaking inside of myself. The day was long, or what seemed very long for me that day. When it was my time, I remember hearing my name called and instantly froze, walking as if someone was pulling me back and forth. I went and sat down before my interviewer.

There then, I told myself that I was going to speak the truth to the interviewer and let God do the rest. I was asked so many questions but to this day, I do not remember any of them. All I could remember was that I had never prayed so hard in my mind while focusing on answering truthfully the questions I was being asked. At the end of the interview, the immigration officer stood up and extended his hand to shake mine, saying good luck to me and that was the end of that day. My friend asked me how the interview was. I told her it went well. That's how I felt.

I humbled myself as I told God that I was leaving it all in his hands and that he would work out the process. Remembering Hebrew 10:23, 'Let us hold fast the profession of our faith without wavering' (for he is faithful that promise) and I can't cast away my confidence, which hath great recompense of reward. God is looking out for the best for those who trust in him.

I can't remember what happened after I left the immigration building. I think we stayed with a friend and then went back to New York City. From that day all I could do was to wait on the outcome. I believe after some months maybe many, I got a letter from immigration and was so afraid to open the letter. Nervousness took over my being and crippled me for a few minutes. I looked at the letter and wanted to open it, but I was afraid of the result. I eventually opened the letter and skimmed over the words, eager to see either "approved" or "denied." When I reached the line that said "approved," I prayed and cried.

I shouting the words, "Thank you, Jesus! Thank you, Jesus!" It was a feeling of relief. I remember receiving a temporary card in the mail that allowed me to work. "That was a moment of joy! Now, everything was about to change.

A Time Marked by Loss

Let me share a few moments in my life when I was so sad due to losing members of my family. At the age of eight, I first experienced losing my first family member who was my grandaunt, then my grandfather, grandmother, mother, father and sister-in-law. My grandaunt died while I was feeding her. She was in her late eighties. I was the one who would take on the responsibility at that age to feed and wipe her down as she was bedridden. While feeding her I realized that she was not opening her mouth to take the food. I called out to my mom and when my mom came in the room, "Mom realized that she died. I was so sad as I did not want her to die, I loved talking and helping her as she loved me as well.

A few years later, my grandfather, my grandaunts' brother who I also took care of, passed away. I called him papa. I was like his little nurse. I would give him a wipe-down bath every day, shave his beard and the hair around his ears. I would also clip his nails with a scissor. I don't remember if we had a nail clip to our advantage. Anyway, I would brush his hair. What I was sad about my grandfather was he had a bad hemorrhoid problem and it was so difficult to give him a bath, but I remember trying hard to be gentle because I know that it was very painful every time, I would dress it. My grandfather loved me the most, of all my siblings.

After I gave him a bath, he always pulled out his knotted handkerchief and whispered in my ear, to close the door as he did not want anyone to see, when he was giving me the usual shilling to buy my treat, which was lots of candy. He knew I loved candies. I was devastated to lose my grandfather. I loved him so much that when he died, I cried a lot for a while. I missed him and was not ready for him to die as well.

My grandmother died two or three years after my grandfather. She was beautiful and very kind. She took care of everyone and kept us all together as a united family link. One day, I was assisting her, like many other times to use the bathroom (which was at the back of the enclosed house). That day, I was assisting her, when she fell and slipped, breaking her foot and bruise a few of her left toes. My heart dropped when she fell. Even to this moment writing this section about my grandmother, I can still feel the anxiety of that terrible day that happened so many years ago. The effect still haunts me to this day.

I remember shouting for someone to help me. I don't remember who came to help me, and I then shouted for them to call a taxi as my grandmother could not get up from the bathroom floor. I was also confused what to do, but I remember the taxi coming and it took us to the University of the West Indies hospital. We were at the hospital for a while and after seeing the doctor, we found out that my grandmother was diabetic and her foot was broken.

For days, we kept giving her the prescriptions, but she was not getting better and the bruises on her toes were, getting worst. Nights and days were difficult for my grandmother, She, was suffering with excruciating pain, and cried all the time. We were all worried and did not know what to do as, the infection was getting worse. Her health was deteriorating as the days and nights passed. She died while I was out. She suffered. So, I didn't cry as much because her pain was a burden and I came to the realization that she was better off. It was very painful for me to see her suffer so much. I accepted her passing. I truly miss her and still feel my love for her. She died years ago.

Two thousand and twelve was the death of my mom. My mom, I was told, found out, she had breast cancer months before it got to stage 4. Every family member of mine, who knew, hid it from me. I was told she, they, said I was too fragile. (I was!) but I still would have, wanted to know. Mom, could have had, the surgery that could have made a difference in life or death. She opted, not to do the surgery, and I found out because she could not hide it any longer. It was obvious. So huge, one could stay from a mile and see it. The doctor told me, my mom had the dreadful disease, breast cancer. I was in shock! When I found out, I was so angry with my mom, for not doing the surgery when she first found out that she had the disease. What else could I say? I just cried.

From the day I found out about the disease, I started taking care of mom. I took her to all her doctor's appointments. It was difficult, but I had to not let mom, see how worried and sad I was, of her condition and the situation she now found herself in. The lump in her breast was getting bigger and was starting to smell and was draining. She was given an oncologist nurse, who came daily to take care of her until the scheduled surgery, which seem forever to take place.

I truly didn't know, how bad her cancer was and thought she would get better after she had the surgery. As my sister is a breast cancer survivor and I thought my mom would beat the terrible disease as well. I took my mom on the bus for all appointments and was worrying if people would shun her because the smell from her infected breast was so strong. I had to keep my feelings to myself and focus on taking care of my mom.

My mom had the surgery. I made it my duty to take care of her. She did chemotherapy at Humber Church Street Hospital for some time, and after, she was receiving radiation treatment at Sunnybrook Health Science Center. The process was really long and mom was not getting better. She was discharged and I and my family had to make sure she was fed and took care of. During chemo, mom was hospitalized yet again, due to breaking the upper hip bone and only to find out that, the cancer had spread to her left hip bone. After the surgery, mom was admitted for a second time. The only difference was that, the surgery this time, was not a success. She was there (the hospital) for an indefinite time. After a while she was moved to the palliative care ward. I have to be honest; I was still in the denial stage and refused to accept that my mom was dying.

It was my mom's doctor, visiting my mom on one of her updates. The doctor asked mom, if she would like to be resuscitated if anything should happen to her. My mom said no. After the doctor left the room and was at the door, I asked the doctor if my mom was going to get better and he told me no, she was dying. I went around the corner of the floor, where no one could see me and I cried like a baby, slowly going down to the floor. I wondered how I was going to tell my sister, brothers, other family members, and friends. I cried for a long time and asked God to help me to be strong. I was not ready to lose my mom, as she was only seventy-one. It was difficult, but looking back, I have to thank God for taking care of us.

She died almost two weeks after we took her home for the second time, so she would not spend her last moments in the hospital knowing she was dying. Mom didn't believe she was dying. To explain, I can never forget and will always remember my mom's face when the doctor told my mom she would die if she didn't do the operation to remove the cancer. She did the operation and everything to eradicate the awful plague and now, thinking back, remembering what the surgeon said, "he got it all". I spent nights and days at my mom's home, and after she was admitted, I had to be there every day and night. She was hallucinating because of the strong meds she was on. After hearing her calling me her mom, I had to make the decision to stay at the hospital to monitor that she was not be given more meds, than what is needed to keep the pain down. I brought my concerns to the nurses at the desk.

My heart is sad every time I remember those words from the surgeon to this day. I know there are many who can sympathize with this experience. However, for those who are encountering this dreadful disease, my prayers are with you all and be strong, in time it will ease to some emotional relief. God is able to keep you through the storms, as he gives comfort to all who ask.

Claudia W. Salassidis

A few years after, our family had another death. My brother's wife. She had a double mastectomy due to breast cancer, which lead to leukemia, that took her life as well. She was a great lady. A wonderful wife to my brother, and a proud mom to my niece, who experienced so many deaths within her home. My mom and dad lived with my brother in Toronto and my niece was devastated to lose her grandmother, mother and then her grandfather. My heart broke one day when my niece broke down, letting out the sorrows of her pain of losing her closest love ones. I loved Jackie and I also dedicate this book to her. She was the best person that my brother dated and eventually married. I could never find anyone else like her. She was always there for me throughout all of my dilemmas. She never got to see my transformation.

My family and I had so many disappointments with cancer and diabetes. A plague in my family. I just couldn't take any more. My heart could not take anymore, and I would repeat in my mind over and over again. Then it was dad's death.

Seven years after the death of my mom, I lost my dad to diabetes. I was taking care of my dad, taking him to all appointments. I love my dad with a special love, as I was his favorite. He loved all his children, but he told me that I made him laugh a lot and he was always happy to see me when I would visit him. Give him showers. My sister did all these for him as well.

Making him food he loved to eat. Dad was diabetic but loved to eat Kentucky Fried Chicken, because after my mom died, no one could make chicken the way he liked it. I would say to him, dad it's greasy and your doctor would not be happy to hear that you are cheating. We laugh about it, so many times and he would say, just don't tell him. I would smile and say, I'm going to tell him.

I had an accident in 2015 and was not able to see my dad for a while. During those times, my sister was taking him to all his appointments and my sister-in-law was making him meals. I would visit him but was unable to do the things I usually do to help him. Dad was in his eighties and was getting weaker. One day, when I was able to visit him, I was helping him to put his socks on and noticed bruises on two of his toes. I asked dad what happened to his toes, and he told me a foot care nurse clipped his nails, and she accidentally clipped his flesh. Dad had type 1 and regressed to type 2 diabetes when I was taking care of him.

I knew he did not tell my sister, so I asked him and he told me he didn't think it was anything to worry about. I was angry with my dad, because he was diabetic, and didn't bring it up (his toes) to my sister's attention. I was troubled and told my sister to keep an eye on his toes. Another day, seeing the toes, I told my sister to take my dad to his doctor to make sure it was not infected. She did, and sure it was, and it was not getting better with all the prescriptions that were prescribed to help to heal the toes. Because there were no changes, the doctor referred my dad to a surgeon and the surgeon told dad, he had to amputate his toes because nothing prescribed was not working.

Talking about surgery was like a foul language to my dad. He did not want to hear the word. To highlight why, dad had another surgeon years ago recommending surgery when dad took a shower and because he had no feelings in his left toes, he dad unknowingly turned the hot water tap to take a shower and after he was done his left toes had a third-degree burn. My sister took him to the hospital, and my dad was admitted. Dad told the surgeon that he was not going to cut his toes off and he survived and the toes got better. I believe that the surgeon brought up surgery because, at the time, dad had type 1 diabetic.

This time was different about the toes, the bruises this time was affected. Knowing that he, (dad) overcame the first toe issue, he believed he could overcome the issue he was having at the time of his demise. Dad was referred to another surgeon and was told as well that he had to cut his toes off to cap the infected toes.

Dad was adamant again and it took me and my sister's persuasion that dad agreed to have the surgery. Dad had the surgery and was hospitalized once again from diabetic complications.

A few days after the surgery, the surgeon came to dad's room at the hospital to tell my sister and I that the infection had spread and if dad did not amputate his left leg, he was going to die. *I thought, oh no! Not again.* I knew in my mind that dad was not going to do another surgery, and I was right. He told us he was not going to do any more surgery and he did not care if the infection took his life. My readers, my dad overcame three heart attacks and now I am going to lose him because of an appointment to have his nails clipped. I felt devastated, as I was not ready to lose him. Dad died a few months after being discharged.

Regardless of my sorrow, I took comfort that he wanted to leave this world with both of his legs; that was what he wanted and we allowed his wish.

Not long after I lost my eldest brother to diabetes, when does it end? I asked myself and I was also comforted to say why not, You Claudia, or someone else's family member? How can we question God when he says he gives and he takes?

Job 1:21: "Naked I came out of my mother's womb, and naked shall I return thither; the Lord gave, and the Lord hath taken away; blessed be the name of the Lord.

Throughout all that my family and I have gone through. I will continue to learn and trust what God has done for me. We all have gone through many things in our lives since the day we were born. But through it all, as the years go by, God's comfort was greater than my pain. God promise to never leave me of forsake me. I will always trust him. Even more, even if I have to crawl through my deepest pain. I trust him more now, than I ever did. So, having assurance when I can't understand my pains and sufferings. It's ok. My love for God out weights my pain.

Chapter 19

Remembering Now A Sobering Revelation

I wasn't sure how to apply for work in Connecticut. So, I went through an agency. The procedure was different, but I did it and was sent to a university that was looking for temporary help. I was there for a while. I don't remember how long I was there until I was given a permanent position.

Thanks to a wonderful supervisor named Nancy Mariano. But most of all, thanks to God, he blessed me with a kindhearted boss who hired me so fast. Knowing I could work without hiding was the best feeling ever. Those who shared the same or similar circumstance I am relating to just hang in your situation. If it's God's will, you will have the same result I had, and with God, you will still have your best at heart. Remember this. 'With God, all things are possible.'

However, for those who are still waiting for the experience of working without hiding to make a living, I will say it can happen if you do it properly. Please note that I didn't say legally because being in a country without the proper documentation is illegal, but what I experienced during my time in the USA was that the opportunity to become legal was possible. I just couldn't say it, and I figured it out then, as I was new to another country. (My thoughts right now, has gone back to the job I applied for when I first visited New York without papers.) *It was wrong then, but at the time I didn't know the rules of the immigration process.* Many have told me it was easy to work in the United States.

But it's not true. When I think about easy, I think about no worry, no hiding and being able to tell others about the situation I was in. I couldn't do any of the above.

This was torturing. I was mentally suffering, having stressful moments where, at times, I could not sleep and was anxious about everything I did. It's what it is when you make such a decision to stay in another country. Just be ready for it, as it is one of the most difficult decisions one could take on especially as the years go by, as countries' policies and procedures of any country do change to keep unwanted people of every kind to not be able to live illegally in their country. *I never thought of the consequences of my action on that day.* However, I will say try to do it legally as it takes the stress off your mind body, and your health.

Chapter 20
A Drastic Change In Decision

A few months after I got to work at a university that gave me the opportunity to also attend school there. I love working with people at that University and had some of the best work environments I have ever worked at when compared with another work environment. It was good to work there. Those days will always stay with me as everyone was so nice and so helpful in many ways. Nancy my boss and I have taken away the notion that she was one of the best employers ever that I have worked with. I also had great co-workers while working at the University, and I miss them all, especially those who left an imprint on my life. Even though I am not in touch with them, I do remember them and carry the wonderful moments that I was left with when I left for Canada.

My only thought is that I hope I didn't disappoint anyone I worked with, as I do so many things without realizing that I could have hurt others unintentionally. So, I say sorry to all if I did, to any of them who know me and read this book.

I was happy to leave the United States to join my parents and siblings in Canada. The best decision I have ever made. Nonetheless, I had to return to Jamaica to pick up my landed paper for Canada. I did that in a few weeks and returned to America to say goodbye to everyone. It was bitter-sweet leaving, as I have inherited many friends and had become so close to some of them as my family. My church and friends in America were the pillars of my strength when I lived in the USA, and I truly miss them.

They were so kind and caring and knowing that, it was not an easy decision when I thought about leaving, especially leaving my friend's sons. A. J. and Michael, who was my god son. After leaving, the closeness usually melted my heart every time I thought about my god son. It's hard to talk about this part of my life, but I would like to say sorry again to him as I did not communicate with him for years. I missed him so much and missed the moments I babysat him and his brother. I had to let go because he belonged to my friends. "Opal and Tony."

He, at the time loved me as his mother, he was two or three at the time and I knew that he was not my child but my friend's son. I had to get over the closeness that I had with him and it took me a while. It was sad, but yes, I had abandoned him for years. I am not happy to say the above, but I have to be truthful and humble myself. I had to call him after years of not getting in touch with him. I apologized to him and explained it all to him. My readers, never ever do what I did. I hurt a lot of people unintentionally when I left the USA. I really hope those I didn't call forgive me. I'm not perfect; only God is. I am very sorry!

Chapter 21

A Difficult Choice Moving Between the U.S. And Canada

After getting back from Jamaica and then to the USA, I packed up and left for Canada after a few months. In Canada, I started to look for a job right away and did so feverish. It was one of the most discouraging tasks I have ever embarked on. I was asked for job experience in every job that I was seeking at the time.

The process was so discouraging and I was so disappointed in some of the interviews that I went on. Every disappointed search was a sad one for me, and I wondered if I had done the wrong thing, resigning from my job in the USA for a life in Canada.

To my surprise, I was getting nowhere in my search and decided to go back to college. I did and graduated but I did not want to find a job in the field that I studied. Banking was just not for me as I didn't like what I had experienced while doing co-op in the field. It was then that I started to think that I needed to return to the USA to see if I could find a job there. I still had landed paper for the USA and could work legally. So, I did just that and found gainful employment through an agency.

While working there, I was missing my family and wanted to see them. At the time, I truly loved living in Canada, and miss being there with my family and newfound friends. I remember getting sick while working in the US, not having any insurance, and not knowing what to do. I did visit the doctor I usually go to when I was sick while living in the USA, but because I had resigned from the job that provided me with insurance when I had any medical needs, I thought he would help me. But I was wrong. The doctor's office would not see me, so I asked to talk to the doctor.

The doctor would not see me either because I was no longer his patient. That was one of the reasons why I decided to return to Canada.

I quickly denounced the thought of feeling guilty about leaving and deciding to return to Canada after getting my permanent status. However, before leaving, I started looking for a job. The process was tedious and challenging, but I eventually found--one it became my second job. I worked for a short while after returned to Connecticut. My aunt had a friend who had a cosmetic retail store, and she gave me a job working as her cashier. It was brief, as it was not a job I loved to do. Anyway, it was good to have a little pocket money and I was fine with that at the time. At that moment, the need to return to Canada was now greater.

Chapter 22

A Final Move To Canada To Find A Job

Regarding the doctor, I understood and didn't hold it against them. The dilemma had me traumatized as I was very sick and needed antibiotics to feel better. Due to not having a private doctor, I had to seek help with some other low-level medication and which took me a few weeks to feel somewhat better. After feeling well enough, I started looking for a job and found one through another agency.

I started working for a small accounting firm and stayed there for a while. After working for some time there, I started feeling homesick again for Canada.

I didn't know at the time that the firm was thinking of hiring me directly and not through the agency. When the manager asked to talk to me about hiring me directly, my heart melted with gratitude. I remember the Psalm, saying "The steps of a good man are ordered by the Lord and he delighted in his way" and that he, God will instruct me and that he would teach me in the way that I should go and will also counsel me and watch over me. I prayed after I got home, just in case I was wrong and after I prayed, I felt and believed at the time that my home was in Canada and I had to find a way out to find gainful employment there as well.

I love Canada and miss my family there. I was also thankful for the medical system in Canada that I did not have in the USA. I thanked the Manager and told him of my plan to return to Canada. He wished me all the best and after a few weeks I returned to Canada. It took me a while, but eventually, I did find employment in Canada and worked for a long time in that industry. I worked in hospitality for a time and loved working there. I had some rough moments during the process of working and was challenged at the time by what I call the politics of the working environment.

Anyway, thanks be to God for my life in him; it meant more to me and I have to clothe myself with His grace and mercy every day trying every day to do what is right in his sight. People live their lives by reading and learning, and by experience that allowed them to base their life on what they read from many books that are out in the world back then and today. I do read books to help me through my life journey as well. However, I live my life mostly by using the bible as my guide. The Lord God is my strength. He will make my feet like hinds' feet, and he will make me walk upon my high places. (Habakkuk 3;19) These words always give me the confidence to say, Nay, that in all these troubles and trials that we are going through, we are more than conquerors through him, who loved us.

I stand firmly and do believe in the fact that God while being in the midst of my storms and in the midst of my struggle and fear, he, God who is sovereign will act on our behalf for the good of us while being tossed to and fro. God continues to take care of me and I strongly believe he can and will take care also of you if you let him work on your behalf. (Proverbs 3:26) For the Lord shall be thy confidence and shall keep thy foot from being taken. Therefore, take courage and have confidence and faith in God as I will continue to say, he will never leave you or forsake you if you trust in him.

I was employed in my former job and at the time I enjoyed working in the Hospitality profession. I was good at my job and did it the best that I could.

However, changing company General Managers can be challenging at times; that was my experience that caused a breakdown of my physical and mental abilities. I was overworked and drained. Even when I was at the lowest point in my prior job, I was trying my best to be the best employee for my employer, but when a body is broken down the way mine was, one's body can collapse, and that was, what happened to me why I had a medical breakdown and had to seek help medically. Among it all I had fear.

My fear among the turmoil was also dealing with some workers, employees and, among other things, it was some of the things I had to do at that time. It's really hard to deal with some people, but in life, we have to, as the world and people who live in this world is, who they are, and whose bad behavior we have to deal with at times. I was experiencing all this, along with the medical issues I was feeling at the time, caused me mental concern. To sum it up, people come with many personalities, Characters, flaws, and disturbing habits, and with what they come with, they bring a challenge to work with.

But thank God, he kept me. However, there came a time when I couldn't do the heavy workload any longer. On this, I just want to say that we have to live together, and what God honors is keeping a good heart even through our toughest moments. I remember trying hard, with God's help, to have a clean mind for all in the best possible way I could. I say to all, just do your best and try to the best of your ability to make it work for you and those with whom you work and live around.

Also, jobs, for some, maybe disappointing in many ways. However, it's what we do to help us to be comfortable to work with others and also work around those who make our lives miserable. However, while we're around people in jobs we love or don't love, and even around people we appreciate working with, they can also try us in ways that are difficult and sometimes make us not want to go to work or be around them. Nevertheless, take courage and do your best as we don't have to like them, but people who are God's children have to love, even if they are our enemies before and behind our backs.

Nonetheless, wisdom from God shows us also that we should never leave ourselves open to abuse in any way. We love, but we don't have to stay in the abuse because we need money to feed our family. For me, it took a breakdown to see what I experienced because I chose the abuse to live for God's sake.

This has been my experience, and I will never want to sacrifice myself for any job in whatever or wherever I work. I serve a true and living God who can and will always take care of me at any time, good or bad. I've learned to trust him for everything. Sometimes, it's hard, but he helps me when my faith is weak. I then remember Daniel 10:18,19: 'Then there came again and touched me one like the appearance of a man, and he strengthened me, and said, O man greatly beloved, fear not: peace be unto thee, be strong, yea, be strong. And when he had spoken unto me, I was strengthened, and said, let my Lord speak; for thou hast strengthened me.

Believing this is the victory if we need to find another job when our body and mind are compromised. God will help us to find a company that would offer better working environment, that can give me or you my readers a peace of mind mentally, emotionally and "for me" my spiritual well-being. What I will leave you with, all my readers are, and this is also my belief and the way I live my life, is that, to have everything that you require in life is being yourself and believing in yourself. When doing all things, do them honestly and rightly in the sight of God, especially in the jobs He has provided you with.

My life in God has allowed me to be the best I try to be, and you can also have the best he will give you as well, according to his will and definitely, what is best, for your life. However, when your life encounters many things that have not been working out for you, just keep standing firm and talk to God in your time of need. Maybe what you need is not something he wants you to have or wants you to go through at the time of your asking, but through it all, be patient and wait on him. One day, you will see why he didn't let whatever happen for you or to you. For me, I try to give my all to God and let him work out my daily life.

Do I fail to give him my all? Yes! Sometimes, I do and have regretted the times I have done things on my own. The lesson I learned from taking on a task that I felt that I could handle is, I have come to the realization not to do anything without consulting God, and if I fail again, when I don't and fail for not seeking his will for my life is, for me, to not wallow in my failures. God does forgive, and he is a reward to those who seek him in our lowly state. I know that God is my answer to all my faults and failures, and what I also know is that I can always trust and believe that he's the only one who can help me in my time of need.

I would turn my thoughts when times are discouraging to Jeremiah 29:11-12 For I know the plans I have for you, declares the Lord, "plans to prosper you and not to harm you, plans to give you hope and a future. Then you will call upon me and come and pray to me and I will listen to you. You will seek me and find me. When you seek me with all your heart I will be found by you, declares the Lord, "and will bring you back from captivity". This scripture has always soothed my mind and given me inner peace.

Humans Snakes in the grass.

I remember coming from work one day when I was living in North York and taking the bus home. I got on the bus and was standing before a little girl coming from school. I remember her getting up out of her seat and standing up instead. After she got up. I sat in the seat she got up from. I was sitting beside a man who was sitting in the seat at the widow on the bus.

After sitting for about five minutes, the man started to touch me inappropriately. I thought to myself, *"What is this?"* And felt violated. I was in shock and thought to myself, should I yell? My inner self felt scared. So, I didn't. The bus was packed, and I then knew that the girl got up from the seat to prevent the man from assaulting her. I turned around and looked at him, and to my surprise, the man kept his head straight, pretending as if he was doing nothing. I was afraid then, but I would now say to anyone, let the driver or people know that you have been assaulted so that these perverts are arrested and prosecuted. I know it is a tough call because we are unaware if that individual has a gun or a knife. My thought on this is to make the decision that is best for you in your circumstances at the moment.

Living in Toronto in the year two thousand and one, I was trail one night by a wanted Toronto predator, kidnapping women and raping them. (I saw his face when he was arrested on a news flash) This experience was a difficult one for me and brings anxiety every time I think about the experience, I hate to talk about the ordeal and contemplate long if I should share it, but for those who have gone through something similar or worse than what I have been through, I will open the door, so you can let others who care about you, understand what you have gone through.

This moment brings back a feeling of nervousness for me. Anyway, it's ok, as talking will help you as it helps me to desensitize the anxiety that captured me with the fear that day. It allowed me to now want to share it. When I remember this phase of my life, I always give thanksgiving to God for protecting me again on that day. I could have been one of those girls who did not survive that ordeal. I still quiver sometimes when my mind goes back to that day.

However, I am happy that I can now talk about it.

Working and going to church in Toronto was the norm for me. However, one day, I was going to a group rehearsal at church and driving to the location.

That day, while driving, I noticed a man in a car driving close to me, and, at the time, I didn't take notice of him. However, a minute or two later, I realized that the driver was driving very close to my car and was stretching himself sideways to his right to see if I was driving by myself. It was at that moment I started getting nervous.

Noticing the action of the man behind the wheel, I made an indication to turn at a turn before my destination to where the rehearsal was. I thought that was the end of that encounter, but I was wrong. After making my turn and taking a parking spot, I noticed the man looking at me through the turn in his car. I paid it no attention for a split second.

After turning off my car and about to look up, I noticed the car with the man coming and turned into a parking spot close to where I was parked. I froze for a second, which felt like hours. After he stopped at two rows next to my car, I noticed the man looking at me and staring at me with the prey of a tiger. To be honest, I did not know what to do. I started wondering what to do.

I had my husband's phone with me, but it got locked, and I could not use it to get help.

He, the predator, just kept staring into my eyes, and I did not let my eyes off him for a second, just in case I had to turn my engine back on. To be honest, at the time, I was really afraid and started trembling within my skin. Then, seconds later, I don't know where a gentleman came from, but he was standing right in front of the door close to my car. My attention went back to the predator on my left side, and quickly, as I turned my attention, the predator that was staring me down took a turn to head out of the parking lot as I realized he saw the man as well. To God be the glory, the man in the car made a detour and looked at me with a facial expression, saying, "You're a lucky girl." When I turn again to look for the man (a, angel) that safe me from a tragedy, he was no-where in sight. God saved my Life again.

After the car left, I quickly got out of the car and told those in the group and my pastor at the time what I had encountered. Throughout the rehearsal, I could not get the experience out of my head. I thought there was no way I was going to take the route I came. I had to ask one of the men if they could assist me in going another way home. The gentleman who assisted me told me that he would be driving on the 401. My readers, I always took the local road home. Regardless of my inexperience driving ability to take the 401, I was going that way and not the way I got to the rehearsal. My thoughts were, the what ifs? And I did not want to have this man waiting for me.

I have to let my reader know that I was so scared and was praying that God would protect me as I have never driven on the highway by myself and wasn't even sure how to get on the highway from where I was rehearsing. I have to tell you, my readers, that God did not only protect me from that predator but also from a pick-up truck that almost took my life that same night.

What happen is that, while follow the gentleman that was driving in front of me and who I was following to get home from the direction he usually takes, I merged from the ramp onto the 401, and the pick-up truck that had the right of way had to swing out into another lane to prevent an accident, thank God that no one was in the lane that he had to switch on to.

What had me anxious was that I probably could have been killed that night.

After noticing what just happened, I was shaking so badly that I almost missed the exit to get off the ramp to take me home. This was not my first experience escaping a predator's quest for bad deeds. I had one back home, three in the USA, and two others here in Canada. It could only be God who could have taken care of me. After the last experience with the predator at my church, I didn't want to drive any longer at nights. It took a toll on me, and

I did not want to drive at all, even during the day, as I could never forget it. For six years, it torched me. That was a long time. Anyway, after six years of mental terror, I came to the realization that I could not live feeling afraid of driving again any longer. However, it was after taking a stress class after breaking down at my job in 2009 that I was pricked to talk about the experience.

Other patients in the class talked about their reasons for taking the class, and I got from them the strength to talk about my reasons as well and to talk about some things I was going through at work that I had kept to myself. It was also in that class that I brought up the predator incident. After talking and letting others know about my ordeal, I started to heal slowly, more and more, and the anxiety started to give me a break. I am so grateful for the class because it gave me the opportunity to breathe again, and I started to drive again after I moved out of Toronto.

Let me open up here, briefly about breaking down in 2009.

I had a most humbling experience breaking down at my second to last job in the worst way. I had a managerial job in the hospitality business that came with many responsibilities, including dealing with other department managers, general managers, supervisors, and other employees. I took those responsibilities seriously and was exceptionally good and capable of doing them. In 2009, I had a breakdown, and I had to be off work and was going through therapy to help me through the mental and physical stress of the job. However, while praying, God showed me that I had placed him, my family, and my life with him at the bottom of my priorities and, therefore, left the door open to disaster. I was too caring and too devoted to my work and people I worked with. I was used, and abused, and had to pay the price with my body. I had to learn the hard way. Due to my breakdown, I suffered from depression and anxiety. As a result of the workload that was thrown in my lap, I had to resign my job. My readers, in working for a company, please remember you have a life to live and if you have a family, they should be your priority.

Chapter 23
My Life From This Moment To The Present

I was losing myself spiritually, mentally, emotionally, and physically. I was so overwhelmingly stressed and suffered from depression and high anxiety. I, at times, wanted to jump out of cars and buses while they were moving with me. My family said I was behaving suicidal. I did not know how to think, how to feel, or how to handle situations after breaking down. Perry had to be the monitor of my life. But thank God! Prayers were uttered by my family and many of my friends-- especially my friends Nicole and Christine, who were with me all the way as my burden bearers. God brought me through, gave me a renewed love for Him, and taught me how to serve Him better with all of my heart, soul, strength, and mind.

At present, it is extremely hard for me to take on any stressful situations, and I must give up jobs that require delegating or of a highly stressful nature. I loved my job at the time but lived to regret due to again, the hard load that was placed upon me. I, however, have learned to respect what God is doing in my life, and I want to trust him and not take on things again on my own. He knows what is best for me daily, and I believe he will work things out for the best of me and any of his children. He is keeping me humble, and I ask that you continue to pray for me and my family that we will always be in God's will. I would like to thank everyone who has been there for me and my family since we arrived at Ajax Alliance Church. Thanks to Pastor Randy and Silvia, The Hos' family, Ingrid and her family, Esther and John, Lalita and Jose, Maxine, Pat, Pia and Gary, Diana M. Practically everyone who, have prayed and fed us in our time of needs. I say thank you and may God continue to bless you all.

I cannot, not thank my Heavenly Father, for guiding and helping me daily, when I do not deserve his grace and mercies. I am called to encourage others, to put their trust in God and to tell every and anyone who comes into my path, of God's love and compassion, taking on flesh and dying for us all so, that we who accepted him might have life everlasting.

My Story: A breakdown in 2009/An Accident in 2015.

I have lived in North America for almost all my life. The reason for my story is to shed light on what an accident can do to an individual and how to handle the stress of it. I am sharing my story in detail of the accident because I believe I have been through a journey that I would like to share to encourage others as well as myself. I worked at a large hotel chain for 15 years. Thirteen actively and two years plus trying to live again. It began after a new General Manager was now managing the hotel, and he restructured the company and gave me a higher position that I never asked for.

While in this position, I started to experience medical issues, which caused me to have a nervous breakdown. After seeking medical help, I was suffering from mental issue. I was referred to see a psychologist and was diagnosed with Anxiety and depression. I was prescribed medication by my doctor along with psychotherapy to help me with my depression and Anxiety, and I was good to start life again after a few years of therapy.

With the help above and getting better, I started to look for jobs again. A suggestion, was to seek a job that was not so stressful. It was then, I had to put a career aside and apply for every and anything. In my search, I found a job in the Food Service Industry.

This industry was not what I wanted as financially endowed as my earlier employment. However, this job gave me the chance to work and to start doing some kind of work again.

Chapter 24

Re-Entering The Job Market after 2009

When I started working at Tim Horton's, I told myself that no matter what, I would do my best, and that is what I did. I found the opportunity to dream again and find a life again. I was not stressed. I was genuinely happy again as I was able to do all sides of the job, and what I loved most was smiling and laughing every day. I got to meet people and got to talk openly about many things that I had tossed aside. Only on the job for 5 months. Then this happened.

I will now open up about my accident.

On February 12/2015, I remember having a wonderful day at work. However, leaving to go to Walmart changed everything. It changed my joy, my dream, my opportunity, my physical ability, and my mental ability; what the day above did to me changed my entire life. I pray every day when I leave my house to go outside that God will never let me go through what I have experienced in this part of my book. It was not easy dealing with Insurance Companies, and I now have an understanding to let others know that when dealing with any Insurance company, one should focus on your healing and leave it to your Lawyer or a family member who has your best at heart to deal with them.

Dealing with them and going through what they put you through, will tear you up physically, mentally, and emotionally. Focus on getting better.

The day of the accident, I remember thinking that I needed to stop at Walmart on my way home from work. Walking my usual pathway to get home, I would never think I would say this today. I wished I had gone straight home. I was walking home when the accident happened, and I stopped to cross a crosswalk that I had used every time before. The crosswalk had a stop sign. I looked to the right and saw a car coming. I was not concerned, as the car on my right was far away. I then looked to my left, and there was a car on my left. I then showed to the driver on my left by raising my left hand that I was about to cross. The driver to the left gave me the ok to cross.

I know I have always looked to the right and the left when I am crossing any road. Anyway, I then proceeded to cross the crosswalk. It was at that moment I heard screaming coming from my right, and I turned my head to see who was screaming. It was then I felt the impact of a car that knocked me off my feet onto the concrete. I hit my head on the concrete and was out for a few seconds.

What I can remember to this day is a lady saying, I did not see her, I did not see her, the sun was in my eyes. At that moment,

I was in shock, dizzy, and confused. I felt pain on the right side of my thigh and felt dazed. I was hearing noise but could not see anyone. I also remembered feeling a blanket thrown over me and being helped into a car. The lady drove me home. At home, I remember the lady giving me her name and number on a piece of paper. However, her face to this day is blank to me. I remember nothing of the car that drove me home, and I could not connect a face to the person who took me home. However, I remember the lady asking me for a hug. Other than the above, I have few memories of that day.

My husband came home fifteen to twenty minutes later, he saw me limping and asked why I was limping. I told him, and he asked me if the lady had called an ambulance or the police, and I said no. He then dropped everything he had in his hand and took me to the hospital. I had a challenging time thinking as I was experiencing pain, I had never felt before. I remember I had to use a wheelchair as I could not walk straight. The hospital took me right away. Throughout the examination, I could hardly sit. Thank God no bones had broken in my body.

The next day, the pain got worse. At this moment, drafting my story is difficult. I cringe every time I read it, as the pain at times in my life is a reminder of that day. My health challenges were troubling as I was seeing my doctor every month because I was not getting better. I was going often to the hospital and the walk-in Clinic as the pain continued to intensify. I also was having back pain, especially in my lower back. I was experiencing headaches and knee, neck, shoulder, and hand pain. To sum it all up, the pain was everywhere. What scared me was I did not understand why I was experiencing so much pain all over my body.

I was becoming very depressed and very anxious once again. My anxiety and depression were getting worse, and I did not want to leave my house. I was so afraid to turn the knob inside, to go outside for a walk or fresh air. I also was having dreams that I had died. 1 remembers waking up with cold sweat. It was an awful feeling. Mentally, something was not right with me. I was starting to become afraid that I was losing my mind. I would think other people were inside my house and calling out my name. I would get up and would look around to see if someone was in my house with me. I did not want to be here anymore and thought about suicide a lot, but due to my spiritual life with God, I couldn't take my life. I believed that I would go to hell if I took my life. I thought about it.

Yes, I did and could not understand the feeling. God, my family, and my friends kept me encouraged. (Thanks Nicole.)

Whenever I was driving with others or walking outside with family, friends, or therapist, I was so scared of my thoughts and the reaction to my thoughts, e.g. (when driving in a car, I was screaming, grabbing the steering wheel, and holding my hands to my face). Every movement had me screaming all the time. I was so out of control and needed someone to tell me what I was going through. I did not trust people and believed in no one, even those close to me, as I felt no one cared about what I was going through. My sleeping, walking, thinking, and other things I was good at and loved to do were now difficult to do.

Diagnosed with so many issues. These are: (Fibromyalgia, PTSD, Post-Concussion, Vertigo…and more) and are presently treated with so many different medications. The prescribed medication helped, and some did not. Some caused me great harm (e.g., having urinary retention and wearing a catheter for one week,) and others took my ability to walk for days. I loved going to church, but because of the pain, I had to stay home as sitting for a long time was now hard to do even to this day. I always need to have a heating bag behind my back.

I was not able to socialize any longer as talking to people and seeing their facial expressions convinced me that when I spoke, I was not making any sense. Before the accident, I thought I was strong and nothing could happen to me. I was very wrong. Cooking dinner was easy before the accident. Now, cooking was painful when I had to use my hands. Lifting and moving some things over certain pounds, E.G., 10, was now challenging. The pain was severe, especially within the left hand along the fingers of the thump, and still hurts to this day. Because of the situation I am now faced with, I had to ask for help to do some of the simplest things that were very easy to do before. (E.g.) Turning a cork on the lid of a bottle of any kind.

Bending from a certain angle was difficult as well. The left side of my body had me worried and wondering if the pain would linger into my old age. My body felt like I was one hundred years old after the accident. I was also cognitively challenged to do certain things.

I want to believe I am getting better daily in doing some things. However, my ability to carry and to do things was getting more difficult as the years passed by. I truly did not know what to do as every help in my case seemed distant, causing me to have once again low self-esteem. The challenge of every day was worrisome and had me mentally drained as fear crept in all the time when I was so fragile in the process of betterment.

Then, a lady came to assess me. This assessor was different, and I realized I had to trust someone, I had to say, I just had to tell someone what I was going through. I did not know if she could help and if she would understand how much I needed her help. She did not know anything about me, and I knew nothing about her, but what she did not know, and I now know that she was God sent to help me. Doors started to open, and help was now coming my way. I once again was able to breathe.

Rehabilitation Journey

The rehabilitation journey has been the most rewarding process. I have learned to take each day as it comes, and I have learned to love myself and treat myself well. I have learned to connect with my past, to live in the moment, knowing I have all these wonderful people in my life. They have helped me and have given me the courage to move forward. I can now say that I am one of this team's rehabilitation successes. I also am learning to manage my pain.

Talking and smiling once again. I am accessing the community, and I am trying to find strength and a new life. My goal is to continue to succeed. I will always be ready to share my story and let all know that you should never take any advice or suggestion given to you by your therapist for granted.

The following are people who have been with me for a long time and have been helping me in my rehabilitation...up to this point.

First, my God and my faith in him. He has always been with me in many good and tough times, and he has never left my side. I just cannot repay him.

My husband and Son. Families and friends. My Lawyer

Florence and her team. Who stood by me all the way. I say thank you! as I could not hold it together without you. My Family Doctor, the late Dr. Sajo. Who took care of me during my dilemma, before and especially after the accident. I say thanks. My Family Dentist, Dr. Philip Staibano and staff who lend a listening ear and always encourage me at all my schedule appointments. I say thank you!

Shelley Occupational Therapy

Shelley, along with Kristin both are from Innovative Case Management Inc., They have been collaborating with me for a long time. Shelley started with me from the acute stage of my Rehabilitation. She has put together one of the best Professional teams. She helped, my family and me understand what I was going through, which helped me to see things differently. Thank you both.

Shelley as well as Kristin has helped me to set goals and to rediscover life again in every aspect of my journey. They have been helping me with my Cognitive Issues and has put in place a Cognitive program, which includes tools that can help me move forward. They have done so much with me. I am grateful and thankful for the magnetic effective work that remains with me, even today. Thanks, Shelley for helping me with the purpose of this book.

I will outline each person's role and what I continue to take away from my many therapies.

Alicia/Alex Case Managers

Alicia/Alex has been with me from 2018. They delegate all work. I am so happy to have Alicia and Alex as case managers. They are my rehabilitation team builders, policing my medical documents, and are such a big support. Alicia/Alex has kept me up to date with the progress of all upcoming assessments, follow-ups, and future appointments. I am so happy to have them both. Thank you both.

Laura Aqua Therapy

Laura is my Aqua therapist. She has challenged me every week by introducing different exercises to strengthen me physically and cognitively. I am so fortunate to have her, and I always look forward to my weekly sessions with her. Thanks Laura.

Nadia Psychotherapy

Nadia has been a tremendous therapist and Counsellor for me. Helping me to understand some things that were entwined in what I was going through. For e.g., I had low self-esteem after I left my first job due to the breakdown I had then, and I felt people who I used to talk to were now like my enemies and wanted to not listen to my ordeal any longer. "She listened". I would see the shifting of eyes from one to the other. (People don't realize that their eyes tell a lot about them) when facial expression says one thing, the eyes never lie. My heart would sink. I would feel broken and would go into a feeling of depression. Others would show a snubbed reaction or come to their own inference.

After the accident, I had people trying to find out what was going on with me, and instead of asking me, they were asking other people and coming to their own conclusions. This infuriated me, especially during the worst time of my life, when I was dealing with the Insurance company. For two years, I felt like I was in the lion's den within the four walls of my home. I was struggling a lot and seeing so many doctors, but none of them could figure out what was happening to me. It took a toll on me mentally, making me feel like everyone just wanted to give up on me. Things only got worse (this was all in my head, I was told by the insurance assessors). Nadia taught me to accept my status at the moment and take the help that I was getting from others. (I was a person who liked to do things that I could do, without asking anyone for help outside of my family). She helped me to understand that to get healthy, I had to do the work to become the person, I needed to be again. And I should never be afraid to welcome the feeling of guilt to reach my destiny from my situation at the moment. She has taught me to love and believe in myself again. She encouraged me every session to change my views on life and, has given me the mental tools to help me achieve my goals. I was struggling with it, but she continued to help me to move forward. I am so grateful to have her as a part of my team. Thanks Nadia.

Kim's Rehabilitation Support Worker

Kim is from Lawlor Rehab. We worked on Rehabilitation, Community reintegration, sensory desensitization, socialization, and an outdoor walking program. She is helping me to re-enter my life which I missed so much, which is my Independence in my activities of daily living as well as navigating my community. Thanks Kim.

Alanna/Reggie Physiotherapy

Alanna has helped to strengthen me physically, introducing exercises that help me manage the pain that my body goes through daily. They both worked to help to ensure that my balancing issues were worked on. Both also showed me how to do cognitive exercises that help with my vertigo issue. They both helped me to move forward with physical exercises to strengthen all parts of my body. Thank you both.

Amy Dietician

Amy has been working to help me eat healthily, lose weight, and change the way I see food and my life around it. Food had become my go-to… when I was depressed or/and anxious. She has taught me so much and has helped me to bake healthy desserts that I have shared with many. I am so fortunate to have her on my team. Thanks Amy.

Marisa Social Worker

Marissa was new to my team. However, she has taught me so much about being hard on myself. She has given me word tools to work with in my life as a mother, a wife, and as an individual. It was a pleasure to work with her. Thanks Marisa.

Rose PSW/Housekeeper

Rose has been a strong physical and emotional tower for all the therapists who was with me Virtually during the Pandemic. She was the one, who helped me, with everything. E.g., Food preparation and community reintegration. Outdoor progress…Healthy diet control… My mood…My memory (as I tend to forget things and events sometimes). I could not have made it this far without her. She was now the backbone of my team. (As the pandemic became A barrier in all areas of physical Therapy), Rose took on more than, what she was paid to do. Including home organization and housekeeping tasks). Now because of her, I am now able to physically do things at pace for myself. Thank God, I had her. She was a tower of strength when I felt defeated on the outside around cars. Thanks Rose.

Dr. Jan. Pain Management

I was referred to Dr. Jan, an Anesthesiologist by a Psychiatrist, who, asked him to see me, due to having widespread pain. I signed up for his Pain Management Class for almost four + years. He was the one who diagnose me with Fibromyalgia, which is chronic pain. Before, my one-to-one session with Dr. Jan, I could not figure out my body, I hated my body. As I was suffering with excruciating pain daily. Dr. Jan gave me a new outlook into the condition, and with his help, I was able to understand how I could manage my chronic pain. Thanks Dr. Jan and staff.

Shira/My Speech-language Pathologist.

Shira helped to guide me along the way with this book. I could not, have reached, where I am with this book before sending it to a publisher. She helped me, as well, with many issues that was plaguing me mentally, cognitively and physically. I had problems communicating with others in so many ways and could not articulate my words properly. Being unable to figure out what to do, the brain fogs got worst. I started being hard on myself and got frustrated many times, to the point where I was avoiding to communicate with others, I felt defeated! Then, here comes Shira. helping me by developing individual therapy plans to address my specific needs. I got through it with her help. Thanks Shira.

Jaisa/Guided Meditation

Jaisa helped me by using Meditation to concur the stresses of my life. We planned and execute various meditations in many different ways. They helped and guided me to achieve a, state of calmness and peace, along the rough and shaky moments in my life's journey. I still use her meditation to overcome days when life frustrates me. Thanks Jaisa.

Things that kept me going

Having God in my life made me who I am today, along with the wonderful therapy team that came into my life. They all kept me going with homework and tasks that challenged me at times. E.g. I have not been able to go out or attend functions since the accident, and I am now revisiting. I am now starting to feel motivated to get outside, walk, run errands, shop, to eat at places I had forgotten existed. Whenever I was hard on myself, they would all encourage me to believe in myself and that I was doing an excellent job. I needed to hear those words even before the accident, as I had an issue of being hard on myself. With God, my family, my team, and my hard work, I am now on my way to continue living life again.

At two thousand and twenty-four, while walking with Rose, my PSW, I noticed a lady in a wheelchair and recognized the person in the wheelchair but could not remember her name to connect with the face I had in mind. God made it possible for me another time to see her face again. It was that second encounter that I stop, got her attention, saying to her, I know you, and she looked at me and noticed me as well. We shared telephone numbers and got to talking about what I went through and what she went through as well. We had so much in common as she talked about being paralyzed and being in the hospital for a long time, trying to learn to do the basic things in life. I thought I had a life to tell. To be honest, when I listen to her, I feel so much more motivated as I also want to overcome my situation as well. She was a God send as I was facing a situation at the time that I would have to do a lot on my own from August to September of twenty, twenty-four.

Meeting this long-last friend that I met when I was working in Etobicoke. We usually take the Go bus in Pickering, ON. We both were going to work, and I remember her as she lived a stone's throw away from me. We exchanged information so we could stay connected. I remember feeling happy that I saw her again. We discussed what we were doing to continue our healing process. We started meeting at the front of my house so my friend, myself, and my PSW could walk and shop at the Pickering Town Centre to keep ourselves motivated to get better every day. I started to feel alive again, knowing that my PSW would be leaving soon. My friend assured me that we'll will be ok. I told her I believed I would be ok as well.

To be honest, I was mentally scared after the accident, and I still experienced a fear of crossing the road. I had the help of my PSW for so many years that I was nervous about losing her. My PSW would assure me that I would be ok, and I would say, I don't know, as I wasn't sure what would happen after Rose's departure. After I connected with my Paralyze friend, who has done so much for herself, I was inspired. My friend asked me if I wanted to walk and exercise with her. She mentioned she could not walk, and the first day she felt a slight strength in rowing the wheel of her exercise bike, she got the inspiration to keep rowing. It was very slow, but she told God that she would continue to row until she could walk again. It was at that point that her strength began to grow even more profoundly. Having witnessed all that had transpired, I was finally afforded the space to reflect and insure that...

Chapter 25

My Love/Hate Story With Ongoing Pain/Healing Loving Myself Amidst Many Harsh Criticism

I aspire to regain my vitality, enabling me to engage in the simple joys of laughing with others, being with loving family and friends, walking and running towards my goal, to pursue my passions with the strength that eluded me to follow a challenging period marked by a breakdown and an unfortunate accident. My quest for well-being encompasses the desire to relish and engage in personal experiences without the need to explicitly seek assistance for the mundane tasks inherent in my daily life as an individual.

I am now consciously aware of the evolving dynamics of my reliance on others for tasks that were once effortlessly managed independently. I also am embracing the reality of my ongoing need for assistance in daily functioning and has now become an integral part of my self-acceptance journey.

Fortunately, I evolved to always continue to cultivate self-love that involves recognizing my inclination toward people-pleasing tendencies. However, as I navigate this realization, I believe I am now discovering that deriving satisfaction from helping others should be a reciprocal endeavor. Lovingly, I have ensured that both giving and receiving are sources of fulfillment without compromising my own well-being.

I am so happy now that I have a goal to encourage and motivate others, hopefully those who would like to hear my story or who need support on their journey back to a better life. Fortunately, I now can have meaningful conversations and not feel that what I am saying is not nonsense. Being on medication has stabilized me, and I am now able to sleep better, and my anxiety is not as high as before. I now choose every day to be happy no matter the way I feel or what the day brings. I continued my rehabilitation with some of my therapists, and I'm now laughing, talking, and working hard. I congratulate myself, but most of all, I give God the praise as he directs my paths.

I would like you my readers, to know that I feel happier than before, and I'm getting stronger and stronger day by day. I am so thankful to my friend who helped me to figure out how I could lose weight and keep it off. I lost twenty-six pounds and am working to lose at least six more pounds. I come to realize that I have to keep walking doing at least ten thousand steps a day. I do try to walk every day and do some form of exercise daily.

I am also now learning more and more about wide spread pain in my body, which is called "Fibromyalgia". Anyway, I do try very hard to not let my pain rule or define me and the life I live in God. With that said, I smile at the moment, as I truly can say that I am now able to manage my pain and that I'm not running to the hospital or a walking-clinic anymore. (I was going to the hospital so often because I thought they could make me feel better) because I could not understand what I was dealing with as the pain was ruling me.

So, I now can say to you, my readers, be not dismayed. Listen to your gut feelings and never stop seeking help until you find the help that works best for you.

Sometimes, it will take a long time, as in my case. Due to me not understanding pain that I have never experienced before. Maybe shorter for others in their quest to recognize what works for their pain and what doesn't. It took me eight years, and I thank all who had a role in my journey for a somewhat life again.

The message stamps the same outcome. Follow your body and your gut feeling for the best outcome.

Please don't forget your family and friends who have your best interest at heart. They will help you carry the torch to the end of the way. I will encourage all who read my book with sound food of thoughts at the end of my book. Please use it in the moment of despair.

I am so happy to have my Family and Friends who were so supportive and have been with me through the good times and the tough times. I will never be able to pay them for their empathy and kindness. Money is not as valuable as the love they have shown me. What I take away from my story is that life is short, and we must make the best out of our situation. Most of all, I will never take anything for granted, as I or no one knows the future and the outcome of our daily lives. Live as if today is your last. As long as the life we live is not lived for ourselves alone but to be there for those who are not as fortunate as we are.

Giving is what counts as long as it is given with a lot of real heartfelt love. Believe me, it makes a difference to others who have so little or nothing at all.

Conclusion
Where Am I Now?

I have gone through many ups and downs in my life's journey. However, when I need to reflect, I think about my life in God first and this special vacation with my son, my sister and her family. With God's permission, a hope for many more…

Now for An Escape into Tranquility.

On March 24, I had the privilege to go on a vacation in Jamaica. I asked three of my friends to help me prepare for my trip. One by one, day by day, we sorted everything out, and I was set to go on my trip. My son and I, got up on the morning of the said date. We decided to have breakfast at Tim Hortons close by us, before boarding the plane. My husband put my son and my suitcases in the car, and we were on our way to meet my sister and her son at the airport.

The highway was a bit busy. However, we got to the airport at a decent time and waited for my sister and her son. They had a slight delay, but when they got to the airport, we all went to the kiosk to check-in. I had not been to the airport since twenty-nineteen and had forgotten how to check-in in. My husband usually does it all, and I would just move my body to the check-in kiosk. Because I was checked in as a disabled passenger, we all got to go in the early passengers' line. Once we were on the plane, we took our seats. My sister and I sat in the same row, and my son and nephew sat two rows behind us. The flight was mostly smooth and went by fast as my sister and I were talking about so many things related to our childhood home and how it would be nice to visit our home on this trip to Jamaica.

When we landed in Montego Bay, Jamaica, we went through Immigration and Customs smoothly and were at the entrance outside waiting for our ride to the Holiday Inn Hotel. We waited and waited, and we could not find or see the company, paid in advance, for our taxi ride in Jamaica. We were so upset and realized that we were Duque. After waiting for a long time, we decided to get another taxi to take us to our hotel. The journey to the hotel was not long but interesting as the beauty of Jamaica mesmerized us, and the driver was so funny, every time the driver talked about a scene that we passed, had us laughing so hard. One of his jokes was about a prison, which was (A hotel, we could book in. However, we cannot check out.) This joke had us laughing so hard that we missed the next joke he was saying. It was a good feeling riding with the gentleman. Upon arrival, the hotel's exterior made a decent first impression. (We thought aloud.) We were so happy to feel the ocean breeze as we waited to check in to our rooms. I got a disability room.

Our room was not ready at the time, but we were able to have lunch on the beach. I do not like fleshy meat, and when it comes to chicken, my preference is having the wings. When it was my time to place my order, the gentleman looked for wings for me and I was so happy that I tipped him for my first meal at the hotel. I was so excited. I was not thinking of anything except getting in my room to have a shower from the blazing heat. When we got to the room, my sister checked the bathroom and was livid as the tub had a ring of dirt around the tub. The toilet base had pee mark on it. I was also angry. Issues of that nature, are a pet peeve of mine, so I wasn't happy. I also wanting a Pina colada without rum at that time, but they didn't have any where we were eating.

It was also dinner time, and we hoped that the food would be good enough to override the issue with the room. When we entered the dining room, the server seated us close to the pool. The server introduced herself, and we continued checking out the menu before we decided to choose what we wanted to eat. The menu was great! I chose rice and peas with curry goat and steamed vegetables, coleslaw, and other side dishes. I had so much to eat, my stomach was overflowing. I usually do not eat that much, but I was on vacation and was going to take advantage of the reason I was on vacation. My sister, her son, my son, and I continued to our room to relax a little before going to view the hotel's grounds. I took a shower, and my sister had her shower after me. Yvonne then searched the television to see if anything was appealing. She did, and we watched a mystery movie, which was getting our undivided attention.

After the movie, we dressed, and then we went to see what the entertainers at the hotel had to offer. On our first day, three kids of a family of five had us entertained, swimming in the pool until we…hours of the night. The pool was surrounding the stage where the entertainment was. The entertainment was exceptionally good. The DJs sang songs that were familiar to us when we were younger. The choices were from Bob Marley's era. After things started getting uncomfortable for us, we decided to leave. We retreat to our room for the rest of the night.

The next day, on the twenty-fifth, we went to the dining room to have breakfast. I looked around to see what they had for breakfast and made my choice. I had a Caribbean breakfast of callaloo, (called spinach here in Canada) and fried dumplings. My sister said she was going to eat it and worry about it later. We were in food heaven and enjoyed being there. Our plate was full, and we left no evidence; ate it all. After breakfast, we went to our room to relax a bit and walked to the hotel to see what we could do for the rest of the day. We decided to check out how we could arrange a ride to take us to Kingston in Jamaica. The task was daunting. However, my sister figured it out and eventually did. We found a company that had a reasonable price that we could afford to pay.

After doing the above, we retreated to our room for a needed break and watched another suspense movie. We got in our bathing suits and headed to the beach to enjoy what the ocean had to offer. First, we went on a boat to enjoy somewhat of a stretch close to the ocean horizon. It was so much fun; however, we had to hold on for the dear of our lives as the ocean was producing waves that were not safe. So, we returned to land. I wanted to get another sail. However, the sailor said once again, that the ocean was again too rough and, was not safe to do so. We went to get our towels to head to the beach.

At the beach, we had so much fun and took pictures. I took fewer pictures; however, my niece and nephews took more pictures than I did. The beach was great, and we had so much fun in the water. There was a small island in the middle of the ocean, which was accessible by walking across the shallow part of the ocean. When we got to the small island, it was beautiful. We stay there for a brief time and continue to enjoy that section of the ocean. Just having our family there was special and comforting. After the beach, we decided to see if taking a dip in the hot tub was another event we would enjoy. Getting into the hot tub was a difficult, painful moment, so I sat and tried to immerse a little and loved the heated water. My pain was manageable. The experience was so soothing and comforting. We stayed in the hot tub for a long time and did not want to come out.

Unfortunately, we had to leave to have lunch before the buffet closed. The choices were great. I had curry goat, rice, and peas with a salad, fruits, and vegetables. I am not sure, at the time what the hotels had for dessert, I just chose something I like after my main meal. The food was good.

We went to exchange American dollars for Jamaican currency to see what we could buy at the nearby supermarket outside and near the hotel. On our walk to the supermarket, we, no, my sister, got talking to this guy who had his car parked adjacent to a house close to the hotel. A young man stopped her, saying good morning to us. My sister stopped and was engaging in a conversation with the gentleman more than my nephew, and I. We wanted to continue walking to get to the supermarket. However, my sister kept talking to the guy. We went back, to see what she and the man were talking about. When we got close, we realized that she was negotiating a price to take us to Kingston, Jamaica. As mentioned above, she did get a reasonable deal and the gentleman was such a good and kind guy. What surprised me, was that he told us he would take us to the supermarket and back to our hotel for free. My sister was ecstatic.

At the supermarket, my sister, more that I, was going juice crazy, getting so many juices that I had to ask why so much juice, and she said I love juice. I was more into cookies and other items that I had not seen since I lived in Canada. It was her turn to ask why so many, and I said I love cookies and when my sugar level gets low, I can have one or two or more if I wanted. We both laugh and enjoy our supermarket excursion. There was a gentleman who picked us mangoes and a fruit called June plum. We tried one and it was sour but biting more into the fruit, it was sweet. After we got home, we enjoyed a needed break after lunch. We, my sister and I talked about things in general and just chilled for a while. The first day, second, and third, we spend our time just viewing the scene around the hotel.

Before going to the supermarket, I remember going into the hotel convenience store to look and see if anything was appealing to us. I saw this cookie and I told my sister that we could go back for the twenty-dollar coins she had in our room. The lady said, a twenty Jamaican dollar coin was worth nothing and could not buy anything. The cookie was priced in US dollars. My sister and I looked at each other and laughed, as we could not afford to buy a small cookie. Have you ever had a moment like that? If you have? All I ask is for you to smile with me. It was a revelation.

We had my grandnephew with us, and, looking at him when they joined us the Monday after the weekend, was filled with emotions. He's so cute, and sleeping. I wanted to wake him up but decided to wait, until he was awake. It was so much fun to watch how he laughed aloud when we were joking with him. My sister's face was glowing as she saw her grandson laughing hysterically when we made a funny face. His laugh was euphoric, having us laughing as well.

My niece, my grand nephew's mother, is having another baby and she carried it well, glowing like a beacon in the sky as all mothers do. Every time I look at her, I have to say, you are so pretty, and she would smile, as I say that to her so many times. Her husband is nice and very charming as well. My son and I are so fortunate to be on a vacation trip with my sister's family. After my niece and her family arrived and check-in at the hotel, we talked about the flight and they went to do foreign exchange. We went to our room for a moment for them to get a shower and a needed rest, and then went to dinner. Once again, we were satisfied with the food and choices the hotel had to offer its guests.

My niece and her husband wanted to walk around the hotel, taking a breathtaking view of the island in a portion of the ocean with chairs decorated with arrays of color parading on the island. On the island, looking toward the hotel, was another beautiful sight.

I mentioned using the hot tub before. However, at first, we didn't know the hotel had one until Monday, when my niece and her family arrived. Had I known when I just arrived at the hotel, I would have gone in to try the water, as I have trouble with chronic pain, the warm water could have helped-- especially, after our flight and the hours we spent waiting for the booked ride to the hotel that never showed up.

We went for lunch shortly after leaving the hot tub and had a combination of vegetables, corn, rice, peas (my favorite rice to eat), oxtail, and a seafood medley, which was not a lot, but good. After lunch, we went back to our room for a nap, because I was a little tired from the sun. Once I was rested, I started watching TV and noticed it was another suspense movie. I stayed up to see the end, which turned out to be the best part. In the movie we were watching, it was hard to guess who the killer was. We managed to watch part of another movie before it was time to go for dinner.

All of us got dressed for our third evening at the hotel for dinner. I'm not sure what the rest of my family had, but I had cow feet with rice and peas, along with a salad and dessert. I can't remember what I had for dessert, as the choices were limited and there wasn't much to choose from. Sometimes, I would have a piece of cake, but it tasted like it was from a boxed mix.

I remember having two pieces of rum cake, but the pieces were small and not substantial. Nevertheless, the flavor wasn't bad. just different from what my palate was accustomed to--but, still edible. After dinner, it was another night of entertainment. The entertainment was not bad, but we left after the wild part started. (We are all Christian. Meaning choosing to be different)

It was another morning. We all loved the beach, which was always warm, as usual, and that's where we usually spent most of our time. The hotel beds were so comfortable that we often took a few naps in the afternoon. Once again, we were at the buffet, looking at the menu for the day. My choice of omelet included cheese, peppers, and a little mushroom, which was always good. I just loved the way the hotel staff made their breakfast. Breakfast was prepared similarly to the dinner options, so if we West Indians choose to have a dinner-like breakfast, we could. I chose to have a regular breakfast and mint tea on my second day, along with a combination of fruits and a dessert of my choice. After breakfast, we would head to the beach for a while, and then to the hot tub, where I did my exercise and got some more relaxation in the hottest hot tub I had ever experienced.

On our third day, I went to the pool to continue my exercise routine, which I love. I had promised myself to stay committed to exercising, even while on vacation.

After the pool, we would get ice cream on our way back to the room. The hotel's ice cream wasn't bad, but since I'm lactose intolerant, I always tried to have just a little, followed by a drink as well. My drink choice was always to have a Mango slushy. The hotel juices taste so good. Most times, when at dinner, our server would ask, what drink we would like to have with our meal? The servers worked so hard, and it was heartfelt. Thanking and tipping was easy.

We went to see if we could get a chance to go sailing one more time, as, I loved the feeling it gave me. My niece and her family wanted to go sailing as well. Just sailing into the horizon was a thrill. I remember, we sailed, as far as the sailor could towards the horizon. Everywhere we looked, we were surrounded by ocean. I did not want it to end. I just wanted to keep sailing as long as I could. We loved it so much, as we were surrounded by the ocean beyond the site of the hotel. We wished for another opportunity however, we did not and could not go sailing again. The sailor, not wanting to risk our lives, told us it was not safe to go at that moment. So, we decided to go swimming again instead.

We wanted to visit our brother in Kingston, but the guy, my sister had been talking to had to cancel due to an emergency. We were very disappointed, as we had so much trouble trying to get a ride booked into Kingston. Everything seemed, so uncertain. However, that day, we all came together to play a card game, which turned out to be grand and memorable. Just being together was fun. I was the one they kept laughing at during the game they were playing. I wanted to join, but the game was unfamiliar to me. Still, my sister and her family let me play and taught me the rules of the game. I couldn't quite understand it, but I tried. The rules of the game were tricky. I guess it was hard to teach me, as they were laughing at me, until the very end of the game. I did not take it personal. As I was trying my best to help my partner win. We helped my niece and her husband win twice in the game.

After the game, we went walking again to do more sightseeing on the hotel property and enjoyed every moment of it. My niece, her son, my son, and I went to the pool. I usually do my exercise in the pool as I feel it much easier with my pain. My grandnephew is such a delight and so cute. He gave us some of the most heartfelt moments and would take my quad cane to walk with, when I was lying down or playing a game with my sister and her family. We were able to find a wonderful gentleman who was able to take us to Kingston to see my brother and his children. We have never met his children, as he had them after we left Jamaica when we last went there.

The gentleman arrived early in the morning to take us on our journey to the Capital of Jamaica, where my sister and I were born. This would be our main excursion for this trip.

On the day before our departure, I had bought some fruits and did not want to leave them, so I ate most of the fruits and felt so happy to have enjoyed the many fruits that I could not get, back home in Canada. During the night to the morning, I started to feel sick. Very sick. I had a stomach problem and spent the night in the washroom. I was unable to eat from the hotel buffet and was telling my sister that I could not eat anything because I had eaten too many fruits. Going to the airport was an awkward drive. My stomach was hurting so bad, that it was hard to enjoy the ride to the airport. I wanted to buy some things but had to stay close to the bathroom just in case I had to use it again.

I was hungry, but I could not risk eating anything, as I was experiencing the runs. When I got to the airport, we did not have to wait long as I had a back, hip, and knee issue and was disabled. So, I was privileged to have a chair to take me to the door of the plane. Because my niece was pregnant and also had her one-year-old son with us, her family was not too far away from my son and I. When we got on the plane, and lifted off, it was hard to find any comfort during the flight. The plane was full and had so many children, which include our family as well. Through the flight, I was feeling really sick and could not even let myself drink anything.

After we landed, it was chaos in the plane. Passengers wanted to get off right away. We were almost to the back and had to wait for everyone to get off. I was pool with the wheelchair passengers.

Let me say, the flight I took home, was one of the worst air flights ever, and I will never take that airline again.

Paying more money to travel to have a great experience is worth the extra cost. I find that cheaper flights do come with issues.

This was a first for me, and to top that, I was not feeling well. It was a disaster. After we, (disability passengers) got off the plane, the chaos continued. We, the wheelchair passengers, were left off to the side before the elevator. I felt so sorry for the elderly, as they, my son and I had no one to assist us through immigration.

My son had to say to me, "Mom, If I don't take you, we will never clear immigration." Thank God! he said that, as my sister and her family cleared customs hours before we did. Cheaper flights have their disadvantage and advantages, but for me, I will never travel on any of them again. My experience was deeply disappointing.

When I got to the visitors' entrance, I was so happy to see my husband waiting for me and I had to let him know the ordeal I had to endure, travelling on a cheaper plane flight. In addition to my stomach issue. I could not wait to get home so I could use my bathroom. The ride seemed so long due to feeling uneasy. However, it was great to be home. Nevertheless, I enjoyed my time in Jamaica. Now, I was back home to reality. It was good to see my church friends and to start working again on myself, now that I have had a break from treatment.

The next day, I slept in as I was so tired from the sun. I was just drained from my return flight as I had never taken a flight coming back home that was so disorganized. I told my husband that I had a blast in Jamaica and wished I could stay one more week. but it was good to be home. Nothing for the next day. My husband did our Laundry as usual, and I folded them. My husband is a great guy and very supportive. I would not trade him for any other. I did my usual call to tell my friend about my vacation. I rested for two days and went to church on Sunday.

All my friends welcomed me back from my vacation and were eager to hear how it went. I told them about the wonderful time I had--and the disaster with my return flight back to Toronto.

I was now back to reality, back to a healing journey. My rehabilitation continues and I have a lot to do. I looked at my schedule and was ready for my first therapist. Life was different and my role was different as I did not have to worry about the Insurance anymore. I could choose what was best for me to get physically and mentally well. I started to look at my life and to see where, according to my health, I had to focus on. I now know that I have to focus on my health and I have to work on my physical, mental and spiritual well-being. It was really not hard, as I still have the drive in me to keep fighting to be independent.

I have made it to this point in my life, and I know that I can go even further. Every day, with the support, I still need, I continue on my journey toward independence. I get up each day with renewed vigor to reach my potential. I know that the help of my family, PSW, Physiotherapist, Occupational Therapist, Aqua Therapist and so many other therapists who have been helping me, I can become stronger. As a matter of fact, I am getting stronger, day by day and have to stay active even when the pain tested me at times. Living with constant pain is a quiet burden that wears on you over time, and not knowing what to do about it. There is not a day that I think, if I could just get up one morning and not have to feel or say, just if? Just if? That would be great.

At this moment, I have to brace myself to take on my PSW, she gives me the drive to feel safe and strong. Even though at times it's challenging. As she would say, you are a black woman with inner strength Claudia, you can do it, and others would say, you have got this or focus, and keep being strong.

I wouldn't have made it this far without the support of the amazing God I serve and the encouragement of my church family, who always take a moment to ask, "How are you today?" Looking back, it was a difficult and painful journey, that I would not wish on my enemy, if there are any. I don't believe so, but just in case. I have to say, please, please forgive me. If I have, at any time walked on your delicate side without knowing. I mean it, please forgive me.

I appreciate you all and would like to say I cannot take the credit all for myself, but with my whole heart, I have to say thanks to those who have been with me from the beginning and are still helping to steer me head on, concurring the aging baton and still managing the on and off painful journey I am still on. I know I am on my way there and I won't stop until I concur with my mental and physical state of mind. I trust my God to help me as well. I am inspired by his words in Joshua 1 v 9. Which says; Be strong and courageous. Do not be afraid; do not be discouraged, for the Lord your God will be with you wherever you go.

Finally, with that said, I delight myself in the Lord as he will give me the desires of my heart. Not because I deserve whatever he does for me, my family and the people around me. I credit it all to God' mercy and compassion, who has pitied me with his wonderful love and his marvelous grace. I will add this to the end of my book by saying, just know in time, you will understand why! Give your lifetime to experience the ups and downs of life... as you peel away the layers.

However, before judging yourself or others, think twice or as long as you need to and tell yourself that it's ok to fail as long as we learn from the experience. Also, don't hate and judge yourself for not fitting in a prestige circle or not having the richest girl or boy as our chosen friends. Remember that there is always a reason why we go through a process. So be patient and wait it out.

The older you live, the more experience you will become. Whether we believe this or not, always be reminded that our life is always in God's hand and he always has the last word and deed.

My thoughts and beliefs regarding my sorrows are that regardless of grace that is seeing me through it all. The people he placed in our lives come with either joy or pain. Joy in birth and pain in death. However, when we find refuge in God, those who believe in him will be comforted and will find peace in him. Trust him, as it gets better in due time. Overcome with faith knowing one day, if we keep true to our faith, we will one day understand it all.

I would like to share some of the Scriptures that held me together in times of challenges and despairs. I hope you can find comfort in these words as well.

John 3:16-18

16) For God so love the world, that he gave his only begotten Son, that whosoever believeth in him should not perish, but have everlasting life.

17) For God sent not his Son into the world to condemn the world; but that the world through him might be saved.

18) He that believeth on him is not condemned: but he that believeth not is condemned already, because he hath not believed in the name of the only begotten Son of God.

Luke 19:10

10) For the son of man is come to seek and to save that which was lost.

John 6:47

47) Verily, verily, I say unto you, he that believeth on me hath everlasting life.

Ephesians 2:8,9

8) For by grace are ye saved through faith; and not of yourselves: it is the gift of God:

9) not of works, lest any man should boast.

1 John 4:14-16 &19

14) And we have seen and do testify that the Father sent the Son to be the Savior of the world.

15) Whosoever shall confess that Jesus is the Son of God, God dwelleth in him, and he in God.

16) And we have known and believed the love that God hath to us. God is love; and he that dwelleth in love dwelleth in God, and God in him.

19) We love him, because he first loved us.

Romans 10:9

9) that if thou shalt confess with thy mouth the Lord Jesus, and shalt believe in thine heart that God hath raised him from the dead, thou shalt be saved.

2 Corinthians 5:17

17) Therefore, if any man be in Christ, he is a new creature: old things are passed away; behold, all things are become new.

2 Timothy 1:9

9) Who hath saved us, and called us with a holy calling, not according to our works, but according to his own purpose and grace, which was given us in Christ Jesus before the world began, when I am going through tough situations in my life and need peace. I remember.

Roman 5:1

1) Therefore, being justified by faith, we have peace with God through our Lord Jesus Christ.

Colossians 3:15

15) And let the peace od God rule in your hearts, to the which also ye are called in one body; and be ye thankful.

Psalm 4:8

8) I will both lay me down in peace, and sleep: For thou, LORD, only makest me dwell in safety.

Psalm 29:11

11) The Lord will give strength unto his people; the LORD will bless his people with peace.

John 14:27

27) Peace I leave with you, my peace I give unto you: not as the world giveth, give I unto you. Let not your heart be troubled, neither let it be afraid.

Philippians 4:6,7

6) Be careful for nothing; but in everything by prayer and supplication with thanksgiving let your requests be made known unto God.

7) And the peace of God, which passeth all understanding, shall keep your hearts and minds through Christ Jesus.

When I need forgiven ess, I turn to; **1 John 1:9**

9) If we confess our sins, he is faithful and just to forgive us our sins, and to cleanse us from all unrighteousness.

Romans 10:10

10) For with the heart man believeth unto righteousness; and with the mouth confession is made unto salvation.

1st John 2:1-2

1) My little children, these things write I unto you, that ye sin not. And if any man sin, we have an advocate with the Father, Jesus Christ the righteous:

2) and he is the propitiation for our sins: and not for our's only, but also for the sins of the whole world.

Hebrews 8:12

12) For I will be merciful to their unrighteousness, and their sins and their iniquities will I remember no more.

About The Author

Claudia has been a very curious person since she was a child. She would ask questions about anything new that she encountered. Claudia's sphere of interest has widened over the years, and she has tried to deepen her understanding of each area through personal research or formal academic training.

Claudia has undertaken academic studies the area of Administrative Services at Humber College, Etobicoke, Ontario where she completed the program of studies and received a Certificate of Achievement, with honours. She has also completed courses in Accounting at Humber College for course credits. Claudia also studied in the Certificate Program of Medical Office Administration at Durham College, Oshawa Ontario, where she earned a Certificate of Achievement with honours. She has also earned a Diploma from Commercial Business College in Toronto Ontario in the area of Bank Teller On-line Customer Service Representative, a Certificate in Customer Relations, Word Processing and Accounting Principles. Before immigrating to Canada, Claudia studied at the University of Hartford, West Hartford Connecticut but did not matriculate as she decided to move to Canada. During most of the time that she was doing her academic studies, she worked at Double Tree Hilton Hotel in Toronto Ontario. She worked briefly as a housekeeper working her way up the ranks to Housekeeping Coordinator, Supervisor, Assistant Housekeeping Manager to Manager by the end of her tenure.

In addition to academic studies, Claudia completed the Certificate program in Standard First Aid and CPR at Centennial College in Toronto Ontario. Claudia has also completed at least two government certifying examinations with the US Postal Services as well as insurance sales representative for Primerica Insurance Company. She also gave time and service as a volunteer at the Canadian Red Cross in Oshawa and the Church of God of Prophecy as the Cultural Ethnicity Director.

Claudia has always had the gift of introspection and could look at her life and the situations in which she finds herself with a critical eye. It is not a surprise that she is able to write this book. I am very proud of her and what she is able to accomplish.

Norma T. Sproul, PH.D.

A Life Lived Inspired To Share With Many

Arkham House Publishers
Sauk City, Wisconsin, USA

ISBN 978-1-967915-59-0
Library of Congress Control Number: 2025914590

Library of Congress Cataloging-in-Publication Data
Salassidis, Claudia W.
A life lived : inspired to share with many / Claudia W. Salassidis.
p. cm.
Summary: A memoir chronicling the author's personal journey, reflections on faith, and life experiences across continents.

Salassidis, Claudia W. 2. Christian biography. 3. Immigrants—United States—Biography. 4. Overcoming adversity. 5. Personal narratives. I. Title.

Manufactured in USA

www.arkhamhousepublishers.com> info@arkhamhousepublishers.com
+1 608 470 3216